VALUES INVESTING

An Omaha Rabbi Learns Torah from Warren Buffett

To Beth,
May all of your investments prosper and may you find true value in everything!
Jonathan Gross

Jonathan Gross

Copyright © 2016 Jonathan Gross

All rights reserved. This book or any portion thereof may not be reproduced or used in any manner whatsoever without the express written permission of the publisher except for the use of brief quotations in a book review.

ISBN-13: 9781505676877
ISBN: 1505676878

Warren Buffett's letters to shareholders are Copyright © 1978-2016 Berkshire Hathaway Inc. and are quoted with written permission from Warren Buffett.

Interior Design by Penoaks Publishing, http://penoaks.com

This book is dedicated to Rabbi Myer Kripke,
of blessed memory.
A righteous man, pure in his generations,
who walked with God.

Contents

Is Warren Buffett Jewish? | 1
The Thirteen Principles of Warren Buffett | 11

THE PRINCIPLES

    1: *Faith* | 17
    2: *Integrity* | 33
    3: *Quality* | 43
    4: *Simplicity* | 51
    5: *Insight* | 61
    6: *Wisdom* | 73
    7: *Caution* | 83
    8: *Frugality* | 91
    9: *Humility* | 99
    10: *Justice* | 111
    11: *Kindness* | 123
    12: *Honesty* | 129
    13: *Silence* | 143

Investing in Values | 149
References | 152

Acknowledgements

I want to begin by thanking Warren Buffett. I had the privilege of meeting with him three times, one time was the day before he announced that he had purchased Heinz for $28 billion, and yet each time he acted as if our meeting was the most important item on his daily agenda. I am honored that he took the time to read the manuscript and gave permission to use excerpts from his annual letters. I am grateful for the generosity of time and spirit that he showed to me personally, as well as for the gift of his wisdom that he has given to us all.

This book contains many quotations from Warren Buffett that I have collected over the last several years. Most of the quotations come directly from his annual letters and speeches. Others I found on the internet or in the many books that I read about Warren Buffett. I tried my best to properly attribute sources. I apologize to anyone if I made any errors in my citations.

I am indebted to the authors of several books. The ones that I consulted most frequently were *Buffett: The Making of an American Capitalist* by Roger Lowenstein, *The Snowball: Warren Buffett and the Business of Life* by Alice Schroeder, *The Intelligent Investor*, by Benjamin Graham, *The Warren Buffett Way*, by Roger Hagstrom, *The Essays of Warren Buffett: Lessons For Corporate America*, edited by Lawrence Cunningham, *A Few Lessons For Investors and Managers from Warren Buffett*, edited by Peter Bevelin, *The Warren Buffett CEO: Secrets from the*

Berkshire Hathaway Managers by Robert Miles, and *Tap Dancing to Work: Warren Buffett on Practically everything 1966 – 2012* edited by Carol Loomis.

Thank you to my Uncle Mark Honigsfeld. He was the one who had the brilliant idea to ask Warren Buffett if he would buy our chametz.

Thank you to my parents, David and Sandy Gross, for their input on the manuscript, and all their support, encouragement, and love. Thank you to my three value investor friends, Shami Jacobs, Shai Dardashti, and David Kessler for all of your input. Thank you to Rabbi Daniel Friedman of Beth Israel Synagogue in Edmonton, Alberta for your input, your guidance, and your friendship. Thank you to Rabbi Dr. Moses Goldfeder for your encouragement to sit down and write. Thank you to Eli Cohen for reading the manuscript and for his comments. And special thanks to my editor, Deborah Vogelstein, whose superb editing was a gift for which I will be forever grateful. I take full responsibility for errors, including grammar and spelling. And to my layout designers Joel and Rachel Greene from Penoaks Publishing for their excellent work.

Finally, I must thank my wife Miriam. She is the true coauthor of this book. Who can find a woman like her? Her price is far beyond rubies.

You probably know that I don't make stock recommendations.

**A Message from Warren E. Buffett,
CEO of Berkshire Hathaway Inc.**

The purpose of this book is to supply, in a form suitable for the laymen, guidance in the adoption and execution of an investment policy.

Benjamin Graham – The Intelligent Investor

I have written this work not to teach people what they do not know, but rather to remind them of what they already know and clearly understand. For within most of my words you will find general rules that most people know with certainty. However, to the degree that these rules are well-known and their truth self-evident, they are routinely overlooked, or people forget about them altogether.

Rabbi Moses Chaim Luzzatto – The Path of the Just

If you seek it like silver and search for it like hidden treasures, then you will understand fear of God.

Proverbs 2:4–5

Is Warren Buffet Jewish?

"Life is not a zero sum game," says business ethicist Adam Grant. "Helping others enriches the meaning and purpose of our own lives, showing us that our contributions matter and energizing us to work harder, longer, and smarter." Grant, like many apostles of the new culture of conscious capitalism, claims that acting ethically and morally is not just the right thing to do, but it is good for business.

The prospect of being able to do the right thing, have a clean conscious, and make money while doing it sounds too good to be true. People are desperate to believe it, but so often reality seems to tell a different story, namely, nice guys finish last. The theory of ethical capitalism sounds great in principle, but does it work in practice?

I wondered this myself. Platitudes and sentiments from academics were not enough for me. I needed proof positive that being good and playing by the rules pays off. Is there an example of a billionaire who made his wealth doing what is right? Show me the money!

As a Rabbi in Omaha, Nebraska I had the rare opportunity to do business with the legendary investor, the oracle of Omaha, Warren Buffett.

Warren Buffett is a business man. More specifically he owns part of or entire businesses that sell insurance, furniture, industrial tools, sugary drinks, and many other products and services. He is unique among billionaire investors. Every year tens of thousands of people flock to Omaha for his annual convention, and investors and students ask him questions on any topic, ranging from compound interest to how to achieve true happiness in life. A quick glance at his investment portfolio would not necessarily indicate why Warren Buffett has achieved a level of reverence that puts him in a distinctly different category from other investors of (almost) comparable success and acumen. A careful study of his writings reveals something else.

In his famous annual letters to his investors and in his many interviews, lectures, and question and answer sessions Warren Buffett has expounded on certain investment principles that he has followed consistently throughout his career. After meeting Warren Buffett I began studying his writings and I was intrigued by his principles. The more I studied them the more familiar they seemed to me. As it turns out, his principles are not new. Much of Warren Buffett's wisdom is a restatement of principles that were articulated thousands of years ago in Jewish sacred texts.

I came to realize that Warren Buffett embodies the principles of ethical capitalism, and his long career testifies to the truth of its tenants more than anything written by the academics. Warren Buffett proves through his actions the age old belief that the shortest distance between two points is a straight line, and that following the path of the good and the just leads to its own rewards.

I served as a rabbi in Omaha, Nebraska for ten years. Whenever I tell someone, the first response is usually, *"There are Jews in Nebraska?"* After I tell them that there are, the second question, just as predictable, is *"Do you know Warren Buffett?"* It never fails. I came to realize that it is based on two popular misconceptions. Number one, since Warren Buffett is perceived as a very humble down to earth person, people assume that anyone can have immediate access to him. The second assumption is that everyone who lives in Omaha knows one another.

Neither of those assumptions is true. In reality an audience with Warren Buffett is a very valuable commodity. A lunch with Warren Buffett occasionally auctioned off for charity will usually cost the winner upwards of a million dollars.

For years I had hoped that one day I would have an opportunity to meet with him, if for no other reason just to tell people that, in fact, I do "know" him.

Finally, in March of 2012, I had an idea.

Every year in his annual letter to shareholders Warren Buffett includes an invitation to principals or their representatives of businesses that meet the Berkshire Hathaway investment criteria. He is eager to hear from anyone who can recommend a business acquisition or investment that would be a good fit for Berkshire Hathaway. He cautions though that he and his partner Charlie Munger often get calls about acquisitions that don't come close to meeting their criteria, and those who have ambitions of doing business with Warren Buffett should know, "When the phone don't ring, you'll know it's me."

I thought to myself, the best way to meet Warren Buffett is to offer him an opportunity to participate in a deal that he couldn't refuse. As a rabbi, what do I have to offer him?

Then it came to me. I decided to take up Mr. Buffett on his invitation and ask him if he would participate in an ancient pre-Passover ritual.

I sat down at my desk and wrote him the following letter.

Dear Mr. Buffett,

As you may know, in observance of the annual Passover holiday, Jewish people refrain from eating leavened bread products. In addition, there is a symbolic ritual in which Jews completely rid their houses of any traces of leaven in their possession in preparation for the holiday.

For centuries Jews have done this by packaging up any leaven products found in their homes and storing them away for the week of the festival. Shortly before Passover begins, each individual "sells" their leaven to the Rabbi who in turn "sells" all of the community leaven over to a non-Jewish person at a "fire sale" price. Immediately after the holiday the Rabbi "buys" back the leaven from the non-Jewish buyer at a small mark up. This ritual, which has taken place in every Jewish community around the world for thousands of years, is known as the Sale of *Chametz*. It is a risk free arbitrage for the non-Jewish buyer.

Traditionally, the purchasing of the *chametz* is considered an honor given by the Jewish community to a non-Jewish business person who has been a friend to the Jewish community. This year, our community would be honored if you would be the purchaser of our *chametz* for Passover.

The ceremony only takes five minutes and can be done at a time and place of your convenience.

The sale will be part of a food drive that benefits our local food bank. I imagine you are a very busy man, but I think that you will find that participation in this ceremony is a good investment of a few minutes to serve a worthy cause.

If you are interested or have any questions, please feel free to contact me at the number below.

Thank you in advance for your time.

Sincerely,
Rabbi Jonathan Gross
Beth Israel Synagogue
Omaha, Nebraska

When I sealed the envelope I remember thinking that the worst (and most likely) thing that would happen would be that the phone won't ring.

A few days later the phone rang. It was Warren Buffett's secretary. Mr. Buffett had read my letter and would like to participate in the Sale of *chametz*. We arranged a time that was mutually convenient and for the next three years, on the eve of Passover, I had the privilege of meeting with Warren Buffett and selling him our *chametz*.

In Jewish tradition a monumental event or experience is marked by reciting a blessing. There are lots of different blessings. There are blessings for before and after meals. There are blessings to sanctify the Shabbat and festivals. There is even a special blessing recited after using the bathroom. Some of these blessings are said multiple times a day, some are said once a week, some once a year, while others are said only once in a lifetime, if at all.

One of the blessings that has great personal meaning to me is the blessing recited upon experiencing the beauty of God's creations. Should a person see the majesty of Mount Everest or the grandeur of the Grand Canyon he should recite, "Blessed are You God, Master of the Universe, who makes the wonders of creation."

The human mind is considered the pinnacle of all of God's creations and, therefore, an encounter with a truly brilliant personality, a genius, is considered a religious experience requiring a blessing of its own. Upon meeting such a person you should recite the blessing, "Blessed are You God, Master of the Universe, who gave of His wisdom to flesh and blood."

This blessing is not dispensed lightly. It is reserved only for those who are considered by the world to be leading thinkers of the generation; people who have used their gifts to change the world for the better. It is said on Nobel Prize winning scientists, mathematicians, and philosophers. The famous Cantor Yossele Rosenblatt recited the blessing when he met the famous inventor Thomas Edison.[1]

When I first met Warren Buffett I recited the blessing.

I felt it was appropriate to recite the blessing on Warren Buffett not because he is a billionaire. Having a lot of money does not necessarily make someone a genius. Nor did I recite the blessing because he is a great investor. His financial success is no doubt a remarkable achievement, but still not worthy of this blessing.

I did not recite the blessing because of his wealth; I recited it because of his wisdom.

Warren Buffett repeatedly says that he does not give stock tips. Instead he gives out wisdom in the form of certain principles. His gift is his extraordinary ability to relate those principles in a manner that is succinct, entertaining, compelling, and easily understood, often employing the use of aphorisms and parables.

On the surface, the principles of Warren Buffett are about mundane matters like investing in the stock market, running businesses, and understanding financial reports. Taken at face value, his principles are sound advice, and those who have followed them properly can attest to their efficacy.

Many ancient Jewish religious texts, Biblical and Talmudic, also appear on the surface to give sound investment advice. For instance, in the book of Proverbs we find,

"The wise one gathers in the summer."[2]

"Harm awaits him who cosigns for a stranger."[3]

"One who spreads out [his wealth] will see a profit."[4]

The simple understanding of these verses is that you should invest your money at the right time, run background checks on potential business associates, and diversify your portfolio. All good advice. However, Jewish tradition has always understood these verses allegorically. The surface meaning has some value, but if the verses are deciphered properly, the discerning reader will find hidden meanings that are "better than rubies, and no goods can equal it."[5]

In the same way, Warren Buffett's principles can be viewed as parables, and a discerning person who studies his writings and speeches will find that they contain pearls of wisdom that lead to treasures far more valuable than money.

Over the last few years, I became a student of Warren Buffett, but not in the financial sense. I have read his teachings looking for deeper meaning, and I have found lessons about morality, ethics, and character development that are consistent with the values of the Torah and Jewish tradition.

This book is not another book about Warren Buffett's life. It is one rabbi's reflection on the principles, the ideals, and the values that I learned from his writings and speeches.

There are many good books already written about Warren Buffett, and I am sure many more will be written in the future. This book does not claim to be authoritative, and it is certainly not exhaustive. The quotations found in the following pages represent a small sample of the wisdom that I found in the hundreds of pages that I read, and in the dozens of hours of videos that I watched over the last few years.

Warren Buffett is not Jewish. He is a value investor, which means, simply put, he searches for bargains. And what is more Jewish than that?

Although anti-Semites have tried to shame Jews for their ability to save money, the Jewish ability to bargain, to *Jew* down the price, is not a vice, but a great virtue. The hunt for a bargain is really a quest to get full *value* for every dollar spent. It demonstrates an understanding that money is only a means. When a person acquires money, he acquires the responsibility of finding the most efficient way to spend it on the goods and services that will provide the greatest value.

As Warren Buffett's mentor, Benjamin Graham, put it, "Price is what you pay, value is what you get."[6]

This concept can be illustrated in a famous story about the last teaching from the great Rabbi Elijah the Gaon, the Genius of Vilna.

In the year 1796, Rabbi Elijah fell ill. Knowing that his days were numbered he called for his family and his students. When they arrived he took hold of his *tzitzit*, the biblically mandated fringes[7] that hung from his garment, and he held them up and said, "This garment that I bought for a few pennies, by wearing it each day I was able to attain a valuable reward for fulfilling the word of God. In the world to come, even so simple a deed will not be possible."[8] As he left this world for the world to come, he wept because he was leaving behind the investment opportunities that only exist in this world.

Judaism views this world as an antechamber to the next world.[9] Our challenge in this world is to accumulate as much merit as we possibly can while we are here. Throughout life we make choices of where to spend our time, money, and energy. That is the price we pay. The consequence of our life choices is the value we get. The principles that guide those choices are our values.

In June of 1996, Berkshire's Chairman, Warren E. Buffett, issued a booklet entitled "An Owner's Manual" to Berkshire Class A and Class B shareholders. The purpose of the manual was to explain Berkshire's broad economic principles of operation. An updated version is reproduced on this and the following pages.

Berkshire Hathaway Inc. Annual Report

There are 613 commandments in the Torah. King David came and reduced them to eleven principles...The prophet Isaiah came and reduced them to six... The prophet Micah came and reduced them to three... Again came Isaiah and reduced them to two... But it was the prophet Habakkuk who came and based them all on one.

Rabbi Simlai[10]

The Thirteen Principles of Warren Buffett

Berkshire Hathaway stock comes with an owner's manual. This is Warren Buffett's way of instilling the idea that he considers Berkshire Hathaway a partnership, and each shareholder should view himself as a part owner of a company, not a piece of paper.

The Owner's Manual was a short pamphlet, now included in the back of his annual report, and includes his thirteen owner related business principles that "I thought would help new shareholders understand our managerial approach."

To quote Rashi, the preeminent medieval Jewish Biblical commentator, "This verse says nothing but, 'Expound me!'"[11]

The concept of establishing a list of fundamental principles is as old as the Bible itself. The very idea of Ten Commandments, according to most commentaries, is a succinct list of principles that are meant to capture the essence of all of God's commandments.

King David listed eleven attributes necessary to "sojourn in Your tent and dwell on Your holy mountain."[12]

The book of Proverbs lists, "Six things the Lord hates; Seven are an abomination to Him."[13]

The Mishnah lists, "Seven traits that characterize an uncultured person and seven that characterize a sage."[14]

The Talmud records the teachings of Rabbi Pinchas Ben Yair who devised a system of nine principles that lead a person to true service of God: caution, alacrity, cleanliness, discipline, purity, piety, humility, fear of sin, and holiness.[15]

In the 17th century, the great mystic Rabbi Moses Chaim Luzzatto authored an ethical treatise called *The Path of the Just*, expounding the principles of Rabbi Pinchas Ben Yair.

In the 18th century in Europe there arose a Jewish revival movement called the Mussar Movement which emphasized a renewed focus on character development. Followers of the movement studied books like Rabbi Luzzatto's *The Path of the Just*, and other similar texts that also included lists of principles.

The founder of the Mussar Movement, Rabbi Israel Salanter, composed his own list of principles of ethical behavior. His list was actually a Hebrew adaptation of the *Principles of Living* found in the autobiography of Benjamin Franklin.[16]

Probably the most famous of all, is the list of thirteen principles of faith inspired by the writings of Maimonides in the 13th century.

When I first read Warren Buffett's principles, I instantly recognized a striking similarity to this genre of Jewish ethical literature.

I cannot say with certainty that Warren Buffett had intended his *Owner's Manual* to be a book of ethics for the ages, although he does begin by saying, "As is appropriate for principles, all thirteen remain alive and well today."

Whatever his intentions, like any work of art, when the artist gives something to the world, each of us will experience it in our own unique way and interpret it accordingly. This book is my interpretation of Warren Buffett's principles according to my background in sacred Jewish texts and my experience as a Rabbi.

Each of the following thirteen chapters begins with one of Warren Buffett's principles. I condensed each principle into a single word that I felt encapsulates the main idea of the principles.

I have chosen to understand his principles about business ownership as a parable. The deeper meanings reveal lessons on how to live an ethical and moral life, how to stay away from evil, and how to achieve greatness.

The Principles

Although our form is corporate, our attitude is partnership. Charlie Munger and I think of our shareholders as owner–partners, and of ourselves as managing partners. (Because of the size of our shareholdings we are also, for better or worse, controlling partners.) We do not view the company itself as the ultimate owner of our business assets but instead view the company as a conduit through which our shareholders own the assets.

Owner's Manual, First Principle

But take utmost care and watch yourselves scrupulously, so that you do not forget the things that you saw with your own eyes and so that they do not fade from your mind so long as you live.

Deuteronomy 4: 9–10

For they bow to vanity and emptiness and pray to a god that helps them not.

Aleinu Prayer

The prophet Habakkuk came and reduced them to one principle, "The righteous lives by his faith."[17]

Rabbi Simlai[18]

1
Faith

Meet Mr. Market. Mr. Market is your partner, whom you have an equal stake in a small company.

Every day, without fail, Mr. Market appears and names a price at which he will either buy your interest or sell you his.

Even though the business that the two of you own may have economic characteristics that are stable, Mr. Market's quotations will be anything but. For, sad to say, the poor fellow has incurable emotional problems. At times he feels euphoric and can see only the favorable factors affecting the business. When in that mood he names a very high price. At other times he is depressed and can see nothing but trouble ahead for both the business and the world. On these occasions he will name a very low price.

Mr. Market has another endearing characteristic: he doesn't mind being ignored. If you are not interested in his quote today, don't worry. He will be back with a new quote tomorrow. Transactions are strictly at your option. Under these conditions the more manic depressive his behavior, the better for you.

So goes the parable of Mr. Market composed by Warren Buffett's teacher, mentor, and friend, Benjamin Graham.[19]

Warren Buffett reframed the parable with a twist of Nebraska.[20]

> *"If a moody fellow with a farm bordering my property yelled out a price every day to me at which he would either buy my farm or sell me his – and those prices varied widely over short periods of time depending on his mental state – how in the world could I other than benefited by his erratic behavior? If his daily shout–out was ridiculously low, and I had some spare cash, I would buy his farm. If the number he yelled was absurdly high, I could either sell to him or just go on farming."*

He went on to tell the true story of a small non-stock investment he made. In 1986, after the burst of a recent bubble in farm prices, Warren Buffett purchased a forty acre farm located fifty miles north of Omaha for $280,000. Contrary to what people think about Nebraskans, he knew nothing about operating a farm. But his son Howie did. From Howie he learned how many bushels of corn and soybeans the farm would produce, what the operating expenses would be, and based on these estimates, that the average annual return on the farm would be about 10%. After making this calculation, Warren Buffett reasoned that it was a profitable investment. "There would, of course, be the occasional bad crop, and prices would sometimes disappoint. But so what? There would be some unusually good years as well."

Twenty-eight years later the farm had tripled its earnings and was worth at least five times what he paid.

He used this story to teach his investors a number of important lessons.

> *"I thought only of what the properties would produce and cared not at all about their daily valuations. Games are won by players who focus on the playing field – not by those whose eyes are glued to the scoreboard. If you can enjoy Saturdays and Sundays without looking at stock prices, give it a try on weekdays."*

Whether you frame it with stocks or with corn, the principle is the same.

> *"Forming macro opinions or listening to the macro or market predictions of others is a waste of time. Indeed, it is dangerous because it may blur your vision of the facts that are truly important."*

Benjamin Graham was an apostate of what was the prevailing philosophy of his time, Efficient Market Hypothesis (EMH). EMH posits, "The stock market is efficient, that is stock prices reflect everything that is known about a company's prospects and about the state of the economy. There are no undervalued stocks because there are smart securities analysts who utilize all available information to insure unfailingly appropriate prices. "[21]

EMH tells you to put your faith in The Market. If The Market says a company is worth X, then the company is worth X.

Like the Biblical Abraham who rejected the false ideologies of his time and smashed the idols of his father Terach, Graham rejected the false god and smashed the idol of EMH.

EMH represents a blind faith placed in the perceived wisdom of the masses. If everyone else is doing something, it must be right. The masses sometimes allow manmade constructs like The Market or The Corporation to inform their perceptions. Like the idols of

Terach, these are false gods that present themselves as having substance when in fact they are mere illusions.

Warren Buffett's first principle reminds us that The Company doesn't own anything and The Market doesn't know anything. These and other like concepts are not real. They are just conduits that require us to apply our senses and our mind to understand them for what they really are.

> *"Charlie and I hope that you do not think of yourself as merely owning a piece of paper whose price wriggles around daily and that is a candidate for sale when some economic or political event makes you nervous. We hope you instead visualize yourself as a part owner of a business that you expect to stay with indefinitely, much as you might if you owned a farm or apartment house in partnership with members of your family."*[22]

Buffett applies this principle to every one of his investments. When he buys stock in a company, he does not view himself as buying a piece of paper bearing the name of The Corporation for a price determined by The Market.

> *"As owners of, say, Coca-Cola or American Express shares, we think of Berkshire as being a non-managing partner in two extraordinary businesses."*[23]

To attribute value to a piece of paper rather than apply your mind to understand the substance that the paper represents is a form of idolatry.

That is not to say that the market price of a stock is always wrong. There are certainly many instances when the price of a stock reflects the actual value of a company. But there are also many instances when it does not.

Being a contrarian for its own sake is also a form of idolatry. As Graham wisely put it,

> *"You are neither right nor wrong because the crowd disagrees with you."*[24]

Any decision in life requires the use of the senses to gather information followed by the application of the mind to process the information. After thorough and honest analysis, if you are sure of your conclusions, then the unqualified or arbitrary consensus of another individual or group should be of no consequence.

As Warren Buffett said about his farm investment,

> *"What the economy, interest rates, or the stock market might do in the years immediately following was of no importance to me in making the investment. I can't remember what the headlines or the pundits were saying at the time. Whatever the chatter, corn would keep growing in Nebraska."*[25]

Warren Buffett has no illusions that there will not be bad years. He himself says, regarding his insurance businesses, "A terrible year is not a possibility - it is a certainty." However,

> *"If we have good long-term expectations, short-term price changes are meaningless for us except to the extent they offer us an opportunity to increase our ownership at an attractive price."*

This is what Warren Buffett calls "faith."

> *"I realize that many of you do not pore over our figures, but instead hold Berkshire primarily because you know that...the record so far has been satisfactory. There is nothing wrong with this kind of "faith" approach to investing. Other shareholders prefer an "analysis" approach to investing...In our own investing we search for situations in which both approaches gives us the same answer."*[26]

Warren Buffett hopes that his investors in Berkshire Hathaway share his kind of faith.

> *"If I had a church that half of my members left every Sunday I wouldn't say this is marvelous look at all of this liquidity. I want people who are going to be sticking around. I want a church filled with the same people every Sunday. That is also how we look for businesses. I want something I want to hold on forever. And I measure Berkshire by how little activity there is."*[27]

> *"We hope you visualize yourself as a part owner in a business that you expect to stay with indefinitely."*[28]

This is what Judaism calls faith as well.

Abraham, the founder of the Jewish religion, came to his beliefs not through prophecy but through reason. According to Jewish tradition, from the time he was a child, Abraham observed the natural world and pondered questions of theodicy. After decades he concluded that it was inconceivable that the world lacked a Guide. He developed his understanding of God based on his observations. Only then did God speak to him.

Abraham passed his critical nature down to his progeny. At the vision of the burning bush, God told Moses to go to Egypt, gather the Jews, and let them know that he has come to redeem them. To this Moses answered, "But they will not believe me, and they won't listen to my voice. They will say, 'God did not appear to you.'"[29]

According to the Jewish philosopher Judah Halevi, this is what makes Judaism unique. Other religions were formed when an individual, like Moses, had a vision or a dream, like a burning bush, and managed to convince a large group of people that he or she had a divine encounter. The descendants of Abraham were too skeptical to follow a man based on hearsay.[30]

The Ten Commandments begin with, "I am the Lord your God who took you out of Egypt."[31] God does not introduce himself to the Jewish people at Sinai as The Creator of the World. The Ten Commandments express the foundation of the Jewish belief system. To ask the Jewish people to predicate their beliefs on an event like the creation of the world which they did not personally witness would have been asking for an act of blind faith. Instead, Judaism appeals to the senses. A large group of people were firsthand witnesses to the miracles performed in Egypt, the splitting of the sea, the revelation at Sinai, and the divine providence over forty years in the desert. Testimony to these events was passed down through the ages by constant study of the Torah and observance of the commandments. Every seven days Jews gather to review the testimonial document that recounts these events, and several times a year Jews gather as families to observe festivals with the primary purpose of retelling the stories.

Perhaps that is why Judaism, unlike most other religions, does not actively seek converts. If someone on his own chooses to believe in the authenticity of the Torah, and of their own volition wants to become a contributing member to the Jewish people they are welcome to join. But it would be unreasonable, even impossible, to force anyone to believe the miraculous events recorded in the Torah, especially if they are lacking a historical tradition testifying to their veracity. It would be asking them to have blind faith, something Jewish People do not ask of themselves.

God called the Jews a stiff necked people.[32] We take this as a compliment. We are stubborn, true, but that means that we don't let others do our thinking for us.

In Judaism, blind faith lacking critical examination is considered idolatry. Benjamin Graham and Warren Buffett call it speculation.

> *"If you instead focus on the prospective price change of a contemplated purchase, you are speculating. There is nothing improper about that. I know, however, that I am unable to speculate successfully, and I am skeptical of those who claim sustained success at doing so. Half of all coin–flippers will win their first toss; none of those winners has an expectation of profit if he continues to play the game. And the fact that a given asset has appreciated in the recent past is never a reason to buy it."*[33]

Throughout history, until modern times, demagogues and charlatans have exploited the gullibility of the masses for wealth and power.

> *"That was corporate raiding of the 80s. The 'escape artists' would buy the company with no intention of running it. Pawning it off to the first sucker who came along – usually the public."*

The speculator is not interested in understanding his investment. He pays a price for his investment based on the valuation of others in the hopes that others will value it higher at some time in the future.

> *"The line separating investment and speculation, which is never bright and clear, becomes blurred still further when most market participants have recently enjoyed triumphs. Nothing sedates rationality like large doses of effortless money. After a heady experience of that kind, normally sensible people drift into behavior akin to that of Cinderella at the ball. They know that overstaying the festivities □ that is, continuing to speculate in companies that have gigantic valuations relative to the cash they are likely to generate in the future □ will eventually bring on pumpkins and mice. But they nevertheless hate to miss a single minute of what is one helluva party. Therefore, the giddy participants all plan to leave just seconds before midnight. There's a problem, though: They are dancing in a room in which the clocks have no hands."*[34]

Speculation does not only apply to investing in bad companies. People have lost money by investing in established blue chip companies at times when the companies' stocks were trading at inflated prices.

It is not the object of worship that defines idolatry, nor the type of investment that defines speculation. Idolatry and Speculation are defined by the means, specifically actions taken lacking independent and critical thinking.

When the Jews worshiped the Golden calf, in their minds they thought they were worshipping the God of Israel. They pointed to the calf and said, "This is the God that took you out of Egypt."[35]

Then they proceeded to worship a golden statue while engaging in revelry that included sexual promiscuity, violence, and murder.[36]

Warren Buffett would have reminded them of one of Abraham Lincoln's famous riddles,

> *"How many legs does a dog have if you call his tail a leg?" The answer: "Four, because calling a tail a leg does not make it a leg."*[37]

During the period of the First Temple, the prophets castigated the people of Israel and stressed that Temple sacrifices brought in front of a backdrop of societal corruption and immorality are viewed by God as abominations.[38]

When Moses broke the Tablets after he witnessed the worship of the Golden Calf he did so because he feared that if he brought them down in tact the people would deify them as they had done the calf. By shattering them he demonstrated that even the Tablets – the writing of God Himself – were only slabs of stone. What made them Holy were the ideas that they conveyed.[39]

Warren Buffett joins the Bible in its warning against worshiping idols made of gold.

> "Today the world's gold stock is about 170,000 metric tons. If all of this gold were melded together, it would form a cube of about sixty-eight feet per side. (Picture it fitting comfortably within a baseball infield.) At $1,750 per ounce – gold's price as I write this – its value would be $9.6 trillion. Call this cube pile A. Let's now create a pile B costing an equal amount. For that, we could buy all U.S. cropland (400 million acres with output of about $200 billion annually), plus sixteen Exxon Mobils (the world's most profitable company, one earning more

than $40 billion annually). After these purchases, we would have about $1 trillion left over for walking-around money. Can you imagine an investor with $9.6 trillion selecting pile A over pile B?...

A century from now the 400 million acres of farmland will have produced staggering amounts of corn, wheat, cotton, and other crops — and will continue to produce that valuable bounty, whatever the currency may be. Exxon Mobil will probably have delivered trillions of dollars in dividends to its owners and will also hold assets worth many more trillions (and, remember, you get sixteen Exxons). The 170,000 tons of gold will be unchanged in size and still incapable of producing anything. You can fondle the cube, but it will not respond."[40]

Judaism, like any system or ideology, requires understanding and adherence to its core principles. Concepts like, "The Market," "The Corporation," "Judaism," and even "god" can be hollowed out and made into empty vessels, objects of mindless idolatrous worship and foolish speculation.

This is what the Jewish sages meant when they said, "Do not look at a vessel, but what is within it."[41]

Judaism does not look favorably at blind faith, and only one who has applied independent critical thought can attain true piety. The sages said, "An ignoramus cannot be pious."[42]

Warren Buffett's first principle demands the use of our minds to formulate our beliefs. To achieve greatness you must act on and maintain those beliefs, especially when it is unpopular to do so.

Warren Buffett's father, Howard Buffett, would regularly quote Ralph Waldo Emerson,[43] "The great man is he who in the midst of the crowd keeps with perfect sweetness the independence of solitude."

In the words of Warren Buffett, "Be fearful when others are greedy, and greedy when others are fearful."

This principle is at least as old as the Babylonian Talmud where it is recorded in the name of Hillel the elder, "When others are hoarding you should disperse, and when others are dispersing their goods you should hoard." Although many understood Hillel to be referring to wisdom and knowledge, his contemporary Bar Kaparah applied it directly to commerce saying, "When goods are cheap, collect money and buy."[44]

By having faith in the convictions carefully developed in his own mind, Warren Buffett maintained his faith in America during times of financial crisis.

In the 2004 annual report Buffett explained a decision he had made that year to invest in some foreign currencies.

> *"Be clear on one point: In no way does our thinking about currencies rest on doubts about America. We live in an extraordinarily rich country, the product of a system that values market economics, the rule of law and equality of opportunity. Our economy is far and away the strongest in the world and will continue to be. We are lucky to live here."*[45]

After the financial crash of 2008 he put his money where his mouth was. When people were panicking and wondering if America would ever recover from such a crash, Warren Buffett went all in and invested in America by buying the Burlington Northern Santa Fe Railroad for $26 billion. He called the deal "an all in wager on the American economy."[46] The railroads' profitability is directly linked to the wellbeing of the American economy. Simply put, Buffett had faith in America. Over the next few years, the earnings of BNR demonstrated that his faith was well founded.

Following this principle has been the secret of the survival of the Jewish people.

The word 'Hebrew' means 'across.' It was as if Abraham, the first Hebrew, drew a line in the sand, with the whole world on one side and Abraham across the line on the other side.

Egyptian, Babylonian, Persian, Greek, and Roman empires espoused value systems and philosophies that competed and often assaulted the values of Judaism. At each of those epochs in history the price of the prevailing dogma soared and often Judaism was seen to be on the verge of bankruptcy.

Sometimes individual Jews left the fold and converted to paganism, Hellenism, or other isms, not because they were believers in those strange gods, but because they sought favor in the eyes of others. They abandoned the use of their minds, and uncritically followed the whims of the masses.

But as a people, a stiff necked people, the Jewish nation forever had faith – real faith – that the traditions and the values of their fathers have true and enduring value. Throughout history they fiercely clung to the Torah against adversity and persecution, and time and again the values of Judaism endured while the fashionable philosophies of the day were relegated to the dustbin of history.

Warren Buffett has said that he is an agnostic when it comes to belief in God. Even so, he has a great deal to teach about what it means to have faith. If more people practiced his type of faith we could have avoided the crisis of 2008 and other financial crises brought about by the erecting and worshipping of idols and empty vessels.

Every day Jews around the world recite the prayer, *Aleinu*, which has in it the yearning for *tikkun olam*: the rectification of the world towards the Kingdom of God. But the perfected world we speak of can only arrive when, "We remove detestable idols from the earth and when false gods are utterly cut off." True *tikkun*, for the world or for the individual, can only come about when we apply independent critical thinking.

The Talmud tells a story of the great sage, Rabbi Akiva. In his day the Romans had occupied Jerusalem and passed a law prohibiting the teaching of Torah under the penalty of death. In defiance of the law, Rabbi Akiva continued to teach Torah publicly in the market place. One day a Jewish apostate named Pappus the son of Judah chanced upon one of Rabbi Akiva's public lectures. Pappus had himself abandoned Judaism and adopted Roman culture, reasoning that the vastness and might of the Roman Empire were proof enough that the Roman culture would outlive Judaism. He questioned why Rabbi Akiva would foolishly cling to the Torah rather than succumb to what seemed to be inevitable.

Rabbi Akiva answered with what became a famous parable.

"A fox was once walking alongside a river and he saw fishes going in swarms from one place to another. He said to them, 'From what are you fleeing?' The fish replied, 'From the nets cast for us by men.' The fox said to them, 'Why don't you come up on to the dry land so that you and I can live together in the way that my ancestors lived with your ancestors?' To which the fish replied, 'Are you the one that they call the cleverest of animals? You are not clever, you are a fool. If we are afraid in the element in which we live, how much more in the element in which we would die?'

So it is with us. If such is our condition when we study Torah of which it is written, 'For that is your life and the length of your days,'[47] if we neglect the Torah, how much worse off shall we be!"[48]

Ultimately the Roman Empire fell, and with it the Roman culture, while Judaism has endured.

Throughout history and throughout life there will always be seductive calls to swim with the current of the crowd. But those who courageously choose to maintain their principles in the face of adversity, those who have faith, will always prosper in the long run.

In line with Berkshire's owner–orientation, most of our directors have a major portion of their net worth invested in the company. We eat our own cooking.

Owner's Manual, Second Principle

You shall have one standard for the stranger and citizen alike.

Leviticus 24:22

Let your friend's property be as precious to you as your own.

Rabbi Yossi[49]

No disciple whose inside is not as his outside may enter the study hall.

Rabbi Gamliel[50]

2

Integrity

In the late 50s Warren Buffett had 35% of his capital invested in a single stock - Sanborn Maps. The once successful map business was in decline, but Warren Buffett was very confident in his investment. Over the years Sanborn had acquired a large investment portfolio of its own. When Warren Buffett started researching Sanborn, its stock was trading at $45 a share. He realized that the portfolio alone was valued at $65 a share. This was a textbook case of an undervalued stock. Warren Buffett had every reason to believe that the stock's price would eventually meet the company's value.

After two years, despite several readily available options to lift the stock's price, the directors were passive and took no action. Those that were responsible for directing Sanborn Maps only owned a combined 400 shares of the company's 105,000 shares outstanding. Their small investment represented only .0038% of the company, and possibly even a smaller percentage of their own personal portfolios. There was no incentive for them to act.

Warren Buffett's mentor, Benjamin Graham, found himself in a similar situation in the late 1920s. He had invested in the undervalued Northern Pipeline, expecting the stock price to meet its value. He found himself up against a management controlled by the wealthy Rockefeller family. Like the management of Sanborn Maps, they had no incentive to act on behalf of the shareholders.

In both respective cases, Warren Buffett and Benjamin Graham fought. In each case they brought the attention to other shareholders, mounted proxy fights, succeeded in getting elected to the board of directors, and fought the recalcitrant directors until the management had no choice but to act in the interest of the shareholders.

Warren Buffett's second principle assures Berkshire Hathaway shareholders that those entrusted with directing the company will always act on the behalf of the shareholders. Leaders must have integrity.

The fourth of six criteria that Warren Buffett lists for a company to be considered as a Berkshire acquisition is "management in place (we can't supply it)."

He says that "buying a retailer without a manager in place is like buying the Eiffel Tower without an elevator."

In Robert Miles's book *The Warren Buffett CEO: Secrets from the Berkshire Hathaway Managers*, Miles writes, "The Buffett CEO selection and management parallels its approach to stock selection and management." Warren Buffett would not purchase a company, or even part of a company through the stock market, without considering its management. "Berkshire never invested (and never will) in a company if the manager doesn't meet the same exacting standards."[51]

Although from time to time Berkshire may employ a professional manager – a person hired to run an existing business – a great deal of the businesses that Berkshire Hathaway has acquired over the years are owned and managed by the same people who founded the business, or their children or grandchildren.

One year in Berkshire Hathaway's Annual Report, as a message to prospective sellers, Warren Buffett included a letter that he had once sent to a man who had indicated that he might want to sell his business.

> *"When we buy a business, the sellers go on running it just as they did before the sale...because we need [you] in order to achieve the best business results.*
>
> *This need explains why we would want the operating members of your family to retain a 20% interest in the business....It is important to us that the family members who run the business remain as owners. Very simply, we would not want to buy unless we felt key members of present management would stay on as our partners. Contracts cannot guarantee your continued interest; we would simply rely on your word."*[52]

A leader must always feel vested in that which he is charged to lead. And the more vested the better.

Each manager at Berkshire is given a mission:

"Run your business as if (1) you own 100% of it; (2) it is the only asset in the world that you and your family will ever have; and (3) you can't sell or merge it for at least a century."[53]

The second principle is that a leader must be subject to the consequences of his actions and decisions. An organization will suffer if its leadership is somehow above the laws that apply to everyone else.

Simply put, "One law should be for you and for the stranger and the citizen of the land."[54]

Martin Luther King Jr. said it well when he said, "Any law that does not apply equally to the minority as the majority is unjust. It does not serve the interest of the people to have disinterested people passing laws on others, or making decisions that affect others but not them."

As a rule, Judaism is not in favor of kings, but it recognizes that sometimes a nation requires a central authority. The Torah allows an optional provision for a king, but the king is subject to certain limitations to the power and wealth that he is allowed to accumulate.[55] In addition, the king is required to personally scribe for himself a small copy of the Torah in its entirety. For as long as he serves as king he is required to wear the Torah around his neck wherever he goes as a constant reminder that he is bound to the laws written within, no different than any one of his subjects.[56]

The ideal leaders are those that are personally vested in the fate of their constituents; otherwise the leader will be distant and dispassionate and may make hasty or flippant decisions. The Talmudic sage, Rabbi Yehoshua, said, "Alas for the generation that has a leader that is not affected by the struggles that the people endure to support and sustain themselves."[57] When a leader is too far removed from the consequences of his decisions, his constituents will suffer.

As chairman of Berkshire Hathaway, Buffett applies this principle to his own management as well.

> "*Charlie's family has the majority of its net worth in Berkshire shares; I have more than 98%. In addition, many of my relatives – my sisters and cousins, for example – keep a huge portion of their net worth in Berkshire stock.*
>
> *Charlie and I cannot promise you results. But we can guarantee that your financial fortunes will move in lockstep with ours for whatever period of time you elect to be our partner. We have no interest in large salaries or options or other means of gaining an 'edge' over you. We want to make money only when our partners do and in exactly the same proportion. Moreover, when I do something dumb, I want you to be able to derive some solace from the fact that my financial suffering is proportional to yours.*"[58]

While there is some comfort from this guarantee, there is something else to consider. Warren Buffett has almost 99% of his personal net worth invested in Berkshire. If he is worth $60 billion that means that 1% of his wealth is $600,000,000. If I also invest 99% of my assets in Berkshire and the stock plummets to zero, am I supposed to derive solace that poor Warren Buffett is only left with a little more than half a billion? It seems that the principle of "eating your own cooking" has a point of diminishing returns. If the managers have more wealth than they can lose in a lifetime, tying some portion of their wealth to the performance of the company may not be a sufficient motivation.

Warren Buffett is well aware of this concern. All of his owner managers are wealthy enough to retire. When he tries to convince an owner-manager to sell a profitable business for millions, sometimes billions, of dollars, and to stay on and continue to run the business, he is competing with more than just other potential investors.

> *"Most of our managers are independently wealthy, and it's therefore up to us to create a climate that encourages them to choose working with Berkshire over golfing and fishing."*[59]

The owner-managers that Warren Buffett retains don't stay for the money. They continue to work for the same reason that Warren Buffett still goes into the office every day – because they love what they do.

> *"We like to do business with someone who loves his company, not just the money that the sale will bring him (though we certainly understand why he likes that as well).*
>
> *When this emotional attachment exists, it signals that important qualities will likely be found within the business: honest accounting, pride of product, respect for customers, and a loyal group of associates having a strong sense of direction. The reverse is apt to be true also. When an owner auctions off his business, exhibiting a total lack of interest in what follows, you will frequently find that it has been dressed up for sale."*

Warren Buffett woos his owner-sellers by appealing to their love for the businesses that they built. He warns them to beware of large corporate buyers.

> *"No matter what promises are made [they] usually have managers who feel they know how to run your business operations, and sooner or later, will want to get into hands on*

> *activity…even though your business record undoubtedly will be far better than theirs."*

Alternatively there are buyers who plan to resell to the public or another corporation as soon as the time is favorable.

Warren Buffett understands that these owner-managers are not only interested in cashing in their chips. To them the sale is about more than just the money, so Warren Buffett impresses on them that Berkshire will take care of their businesses like no other corporation.

> *"The sellers' business represents the creative work of a lifetime and remains an integral part of their personality and sense of being."*

This is what the Jewish sage, Antigonos of Socho, meant when he said, "Do not be like a servant who serves his master for the sake of receiving a reward, but be rather like a servant who serves his master without the express intention of receiving a reward."[60] Antigonos did not mean that we should work for free, but rather we should serve God more out of love for Him, than out of fear of Him.

In the earliest story of mankind in the Bible, after Adam ate of the forbidden fruit, God said to him, "Cursed be the ground because of you….Thorns and thistles shall it sprout for you, and your food shall be the grasses of the field; by the sweat of your brow shall you eat your bread."[61]

The classic understanding of the curse is that, before the sin, the fruits of the Garden of Eden grew without any effort or assistance from man, and Adam and Eve lived lives of leisure without toil. The punishment was that now they had to go to work.

The sages of the Talmud offer an alternative understanding. At first God proclaimed, "Cursed be the ground because of you...and your food will be the grasses of the field." Upon hearing this terrible decree Adam broke down in anguish. Seeing Adam's pain, God softened the blow and comforted Adam with the assurance, "By the sweat of your brow you can eat bread."[62]

The curse was that Adam would have to eat grass like an animal. But the curse came with a great blessing. Adam could once again eat with the dignity of a man as he did before the sin. All he needs to do is apply the sweat of his brow and the work of his hands.

While many perceive work to be the greatest curse that was ever given to mankind, fortunate are those who understand that it is, in fact, the greatest blessing.

The sages taught that there are "those who toil and receive reward and there are those who toil and receive no reward."[63] Both may be paid money for their services, but those who love their work receive additional reward in the satisfaction of a job well done.

Warren Buffett looks for people who love what they do. Like him, they tap dance to work. They are people of integrity. They have no problem eating their own cooking. They can be trusted with leadership because they are not motivated only by the pursuit of money. They value their work, and they are proud of the consequences of their actions.

Our long-term economic goal (subject to some qualifications mentioned later) is to maximize Berkshire's average annual rate of gain in intrinsic business value on a per-share basis. We do not measure the economic significance or performance of Berkshire by its size; we measure by per-share progress. We are certain that the rate of per-share progress will diminish in the future – a greatly enlarged capital base will see to that. But we will be disappointed if our rate does not exceed that of the average large American corporation.

Owner's Manual, Third Principle

Not because you are more numerous than all the peoples did Hashem desire you and choose you, for you are the fewest of all the peoples.

Deuteronomy 7:7

The stone the builders rejected has become the main cornerstone.

Psalms 118:22

A small vessel when you need it is to you like a large vessel.

Rabbi Hanina[64]

3
Quality

In 1937 a ten-year-old boy and his family fled Germany to escape the Nazis and landed in a small Jewish settlement in what was then called Palestine. The settlement was Tel Aviv; the boy, Stef Wertheimer.

Stef dropped out of school at sixteen and began working for a camera repair shop. Although he did not have a formal education, he loved to learn, and he was born with a gift of technical genius.

When World War II broke out he joined the British Air Force and served as an optical equipment technician. After the war, Stef joined the Palmach, the elite fighting force of the paramilitary group that later became the Israel Defense Forces. During Israel's War of Independence he served as a technical officer and worked on the improvement of the IDF's artillery.

In 1952 he settled in the Israeli city of Netanya and started a small business designing and selling cutting tools. He ran the business out of a small wooden garage in his backyard. He named the company Iscar.

Over the next fifty years Iscar grew and became a leader in the production of industrial tools. Today Iscar has representation in over sixty countries and includes carmakers Ford and General Motors among its clients.

In 2006 Warren Buffett bought an 80% stake in Iscar for over $4 billion.

He closed the deal on July 5th of that year. One week later, on July 12th, Hezbollah started what came to be known as the Second Lebanon War. Thousands of rockets were fired from Lebanon and rained down on Northern Israel. Iscar's main facility is located less than eight miles from the Israel-Lebanon border.

During the war, Warren Buffett was asked in an interview whether he had any regrets about purchasing Iscar. "Absolutely none!" he said. Even if a missile were to destroy the facility Iscar could rebuild. The value of the company is not in the factory, "it is in the talented employees and management."

Iscar was his first major investment outside of the United States. While the foolish Jew-haters of the world are trying to divest from Israel, Warren Buffett invested in Israel.

What did he find in Israel that he has not yet found in larger countries throughout Europe, Asia, or South America?

"Others come to the Middle East looking for oil. We came looking for brains and talent. And you've got that in Israel. Look at where Israel was sixty years ago and look where it is today. What country in the world has made that kind of progress in such a short time? When you think about it, where has any group of 6 or 7 million people made that kind of progress anywhere in the world?"[65]

Warren Buffett's third principle is to judge not by size, but by per share progress. Otherwise stated, whatever the quantity, you should always demand quality.

The Jewish people understand this principle as much as anyone else. Iscar's products are a perfect metaphor for Israel's role on the world stage, and the Jewish people's role throughout history.

> *"ISCAR's products are small, consumable cutting tools that are used in conjunction with large and expensive machine tools. It's a business [that] develops tools that make their customers' machines more productive. The result: ISCAR makes money because it enables its customers to make more money. There is no better recipe for continued success."*[66]

Natan Sharansky, the former Soviet dissident and Jewish hero, tells a story about a Chinese man who once asked, "Why does the world hear so much about Israel when there are only fifty million Jews?"[67]

In reality Israel is a small country of about 7 million people, and the Jews are a small dispersed nation of about 14 million worldwide. Some have quipped that the Jewish people amount to the same number as the margin of error in the Chinese census. Yet despite our modest numbers we make a big impact in finance, art, culture, science, technology, and politics. The contributions of the Jewish people have advanced society and made the world better for everyone.

Perhaps that is the reason why there was a Biblical prohibition against taking a direct census.[68] The Torah wants to teach that we should not put too much stock in our numbers.

Bigger is not always better.

Warren Buffett even cautions that sometimes big can be a liability.

> *"The major problem we face is a growing capital base. You've heard that from us before, but this problem, like age, grows in significance each year."*

On the other hand, being big has its advantages. Warren Buffett contrasts how easy it was to have great returns percentage-wise when he only had fifty thousand in capital. Having billions makes for harder returns, but is obviously preferable.

Continuing with the age metaphor,

> *"Just as with age, it's better to have this problem continue to grow rather than to have it 'solved.'"*[69]

When Warren Buffett searches for investment opportunities he doesn't judge a company by its size. He searches for companies with high per share value. Two companies of comparable quantity can vary significantly in value based on their respective quality.

A quality company, product, or person can be recognized by a certain efficiency of spirit. Substance not fluff. Maximum weight per unit.

Quality can be applied as aptly to the ephemeral as it can be to the material.

When Moses set up the first Jewish court system after the Exodus, his father-in-law Yitro gave Moses some unsolicited advice. Yitro suggested that Moses delegate his heavy case load to a system of lower courts, and Moses's judgement should be reserved for only the *"big"* cases.

Moses implemented his father-in-law's suggestion, with one subtle variation. Moses established a hierarchical court system with Moses serving as chief justice, but instead of presiding over only the "big" cases, Moses chose to preside over the "hard" cases.[70]

The trial of OJ Simpson was a "big" case, but as far as legal theory is concerned, it was not a "hard" case. It was a murder case with a celebrity defendant. Future legal scholars will not study the OJ case for its groundbreaking significance in legal theory. The cases that set legal precedent are usually cases of unknown litigants who by chance become engaged in an unprecedented dispute. Those are the hard cases that went to Moses and those are the cases that go to our Supreme Court. *Big* does not imply hard.

The principle of quality should also be applied to the way that we speak.

Often, but not always, the length of a speech and the quality of its content are inversely proportional. There is a humorous quotation attributed to Winston Churchill, "If I am to speak for a few minutes I require a week to prepare. If I am to speak for an hour, I am ready now."

The Talmud records the praises given to Rabbi Eliezer Ben Yaakov because his teachings were terse and to the point.[71]

In the Passover Haggadah we recount the teaching of Rabbi Yehudah who made an acronym for the ten plagues, "Ditzach Adash Biachav." The Acronym is almost as hard to remember as the ten plagues themselves. Perhaps the lesson is that Rabbi Yehuda could convey an idea using only three words when everyone else required ten. The sages valued his economy of language.

Actions can also have quality. Rabbi Yehudah the Nasi, the editor of the Mishnah, taught, "Be as meticulous with a minor commandment as with a major one, for you don't know the reward for each mitzvah."[72] Don't underestimate the potential impact of even the smallest deed. As the verse says, "How good is a thing done in its proper time!"[73]

Most important, we have the power to add quality to life.

King Solomon told his son that if he engaged in Torah study his son would be guaranteed "length of days."[74] He did not say, "a long life." That would be "many days," not "length of days." Nobody on earth can guarantee a long life. The guarantee of "length of days" means that if you engage in the study of Torah and other virtuous pursuits, regardless of the quantity of your days, all of the days that you have will be long and meaningful. They will be quality days.

Rudyard Kipling wrote that a true man is one who can "fill the unforgiving minute with sixty seconds of distance run."

The quantity of our days is in God's hands. The quality of our days is in ours.

Our preference would be to reach our goal by directly owning a diversified group of businesses that generate cash and consistently earn above-average returns on capital. Our second choice is to own parts of similar businesses, attained primarily through purchases of marketable common stocks by our insurance subsidiaries. The price and availability of businesses and the need for insurance capital determine any given year's capital allocation.

Owner's Manual, Fourth Principle

The righteous walks in his simplicity, fortunate are his children after him.

Proverbs 20:7

One should always teach his son a craft that is clean and simple.

Bar Kapparah[75]

What's this?

The Simple Son

4
Simplicity

Rose Blumkin was one of Warren Buffett's heroes. Her legendary life story is an iconic tale, an example *par excellence* of the American dream. As a girl she fled Russia leaving behind poverty and persecution. She trekked thousands of miles by land and by sea to arrive on the shores of America, the land of freedom and opportunity, settling in Omaha, Nebraska.

She arrived in America without a penny to her name. She worked hard and saved until she was able to start her own small business selling furniture out of her home. Eventually she opened a store, The Nebraska Furniture Mart, and she dedicated every waking hour to her business. She went head to head with the big corporate retailers, and with her tenacity and innate business acumen she triumphed.

In 1983, at the age of ninety, she sold her business, the Nebraska Furniture Mart, to Warren Buffett for $60 million. She and her family continued to operate it until her death in 1998 at the age of 104. She continued to work at the Mart every day, almost until the day she died.

She was a shrewd business woman, tough as nails. She lived and breathed her business. Legend has it, she never really learned proper English, nor could she read or write, but she could take measurements, add tax, and give you a discount all calculated within seconds in her head. She knew every square inch of her store, every piece of merchandise, and the price that she paid for it.

A few years after she sold her company to Warren Buffett, she had a disagreement with her grandsons, who were at that time running the business. One can imagine the challenges that they faced managing the multimillion dollar business in the shadow of their legendary, and very opinionated, grandmother manager emeritus. After a period of tension, they acted to override one of her unilateral decisions. This was the last straw. Rose stormed out of the store, demanding $96,000 in unpaid vacation days.

Before long, she purchased a warehouse across the street and converted it into a furniture store of her own, "Mrs. B's," competing with the Furniture Mart by undercutting their prices. After just three months, "Mrs. B's" grossed $265 million in sales. After just two years, she was the third most profitable carpet retailer in Omaha.

Finally, Warren Buffett stepped in. He came to her with flowers and a box of See's Candy. He offered her $4.94 million for Mrs. B's. She missed the Furniture Mart, and missed her family. She accepted the offer (earning her a profit of almost $3 million on her initial investment) and came back to the Mart. She did this at the age of ninety-nine. This time Warren Buffett made her sign a non-compete clause with a term limit that he hoped would outlast her.

Warren Buffett sets the compensation for the managers of all the Berkshire companies. At a time when Warren Buffett paid himself an annual salary of $100,000, he paid Mrs. B $300,000.

There is hardly a home in Omaha that does not contain furniture from The Mart, which means that almost everyone in Omaha was a customer of Mrs. B. Although I did not know her personally, I moved to Omaha a few years after she died, I heard dozens of people tell me of their personal encounters with her. Everyone has a story about Mrs. B.

When I first met with Warren Buffett I presented him with a challah baked in the kitchen of the Rose Blumkin Jewish Home for the aged. When I told him where the challah came from he smiled, reached into his desk, and pulled out the original contract that he signed with Rose Blumkin when he purchased the Furniture Mart in 1983. The contract was one page long, and most of the page contained signatures of the Blumkin family. He told me that the entire transaction cost him less than $1,800 in lawyers' fees. He trusted her implicitly. "I asked her if she owned the buildings outright and if she owed any money. She told me 'yes' and 'no' so we shook hands and we had a deal."

Rose Blumkin didn't have any formal education, but she had a number of honorary degrees from universities around the country. In her acceptance speech when she received her honorary degree from Omaha's Creighton University, her advice to graduating seniors was, "First, honesty. Second hard work. Next, if you don't get the job you want right away, tell them you'll take anything. If you're good, they will keep you."[76]

Her advice, just like her deal with Warren Buffett, exemplifies Warren Buffett's fourth principle, simplicity.

Simplicity | 53

Ask Warren Buffett what his investment secret is and he will tell you. It is not complicated. Buy really good businesses, or pieces of really good businesses. It's that simple. How does he define a good business?

> "Our acquisition preferences run towards businesses that generate cash, not those that consume it."[77]

He admired Rose Blumkin's simplicity. He trusted her because he knew where he stood with her. She told it like it was. She applied the principle of simplicity to every aspect of her life.

"You got about two inches outside of her circle of competence, she didn't even want to talk to you about it. She knew exactly what she was good at."[78]

Warren Buffett is a firm believer in staying within your circle of competence.

> "We try to exert a Ted Williams kind of discipline. In his book, the science of hitting Ted explains that he carved the strike zone into seventy-seven cells each the size of a baseball. Swinging at balls only in his best cells, he knew, would allow him to bat .400. Reaching for balls in his worst cells, the lower outside corner of the strike zone, would reduce him to .230. In other words, waiting for the fat pitch would mean a trip to the Hall of Fame and swinging indiscriminately would be a ticket back to the minors."[79]

When Warren Buffett looks to invest he looks for companies that he finds easy to understand, and are within his circle of competence. A casual perusal of Berkshire's holdings reveals a collection of companies in a wide variety of fields. Companies like

Coke, Nebraska Furniture Mart, and Iscar sell soft drinks, furniture, and tools, respectively. They have little in common, but they are all leaders in industries that can be easily explained.

When asked why he invested in Gillette, he said, "Men's beards grow all night. I make money while they sleep. Women have two legs, that's even better."[80]

Conversely, Warren Buffett sat out the dotcom fever of the late 90s, and to this day he shies away from companies like Facebook, Amazon, and Google. He considers social media, online retailers, and search engines to be outside of his circle of competence. He sticks to industries that he understands, and he is not afraid to say that he does not understand something.

Warren Buffett doesn't prescribe as a rule that you must have a diversified portfolio. Diversity is not in and of itself a magic formula. The essential element is a simple understanding of all of your investments. "One bet soundly considered is preferable to many poorly understood."[81]

Charlie Munger is fond of quoting Albert Einstein who said, "if you can't explain it to a six year old, you don't really understand it yourself."[82]

The Passover Seder is a meal held annually to celebrate the anniversary of the Exodus from Egypt. The purpose of the Passover Seder is to "Tell your child on that day, saying 'It is because of this that God acted for me when I came forth out of Egypt.'"[83] The ancient Jewish sages compiled The Passover Haggadah, a book of texts and rituals designed to stimulate lively discussion and guide each family through the challenging task of passing on the legacy to the next generation.

Recognizing that each child learns differently, the sages included a section that speaks of four sons; the wise son, the wicked son, the simple son, and the son who does not know how to ask questions. Each of the four sons is meant to represent a different educational paradigm. Each one asks a different question based on his personality, and the Haggadah provides different answers to each question. The section of the four sons is meant to teach us that no two children are the same, and we should "teach each child according to their own way."[84]

The wise son asks, "What are the laws, statutes, and ordinances that God has commanded you?"

It is widely assumed that the wise son represents the ideal child, in contrast to the wicked son. But upon closer examination, the wise son's question completely misses the point of the seder. He focuses on the rituals associated with the Passover holiday, but fails to accomplish the main task, to retell the story of the Exodus from Egypt.

The rituals are only there to prompt a retelling of the story. A Passover seder with only "wise" sons could go on all night discussing the details of how much unleavened bread to eat, how many cups of wine to drink, and how bitter the herbs should be, and by the time the sun comes up the words "slavery" and "Egypt" have not even been mentioned.

It is the third son, the simple son, who asks the most penetrating question. He asks, "What's this?" The simple son asks the most important question of all. He asks a simple direct question, and receives a simple direct answer. "Say to [the simple son] 'By strength of hand did God bring us out from Egypt, from the house of bondage.'"[85] Because of his question the seder is a complete success. Mission accomplished.

Unfortunately, sometimes the simple direct question goes unasked.

Sometimes the simple question goes unasked because we are too embarrassed to ask it. Like the tale of the emperor's new clothes, nobody wants to ask a question that will make him appear foolish in the eyes of others. The Talmudic sage Hillel warns us, "One who fears embarrassment will not learn."[86]

The third son of the Passover Haggadah is called the simple son, which is a poor translation of the original Hebrew. The Hebrew word used in the Haggadah is the word 'tam." This same word is used in the Bible to describe Noah[87], Abraham[88], Jacob[89], and Job[90]. None of these were 'simple' men. The word 'tam' really means 'pure.'

The Torah contrasts the differences between the twins, Jacob and Esau. Esau is described as a man who "knew how to trap," while his brother Jacob is described as "tam."[91] According to the Biblical commentator Rashi, when the Bible tells us that Esau knew how to "trap" with his mouth, it means that he was deceptive. By contrast, Jacob was 'tam' which means, "He was not adept at [deception]. His mouth and his ear were as one."

The ancient translator Onkelos translated the word 'tam' as 'shalim' – the Aramaic word that means 'wholesome.'

In desperate attempts to present a novel new approach to an old subject, people will sometimes concoct complicated, convoluted, and often counterintuitive analyses that try to deceive others, and sometimes themselves, that black is white, yes is no, or good is bad.

At one point, certain analysts insisted that junk bonds were a safe investment because, they reasoned, huge debt and the fear of imminent default would incentivize the issuers to focus their efforts as never before. Warren Buffett ridiculed this twisted logic with a parable.

> *"A dagger mounted on the steering wheel of a car could be expected to make its driver proceed with intensified care. But another certain consequence would be if the car hit even the tiniest pothole there would be an accident."*[92]

The inclination and desire to see the underdog triumph can lead to perversions of reality and raise false hopes. It can make people believe that anything is possible, no matter how unlikely or improbable.

> *"People are brought up watching movies about princes that are trapped as toads until a princess comes along and kisses them. Some manager investors think that their managerial 'kisses' will turn around these toad companies and make them princes."*

But as Buffett often says, "Turn-arounds seldom turn."

Similarly, "I would rather be certain of a good result than hopeful of a great one."

There is no virtue in inventing unrealistic expectations to create false optimism. Intellectual acrobatics used to distort reality are nothing more than self-deception. The person who speaks only what he knows to be true in his heart has the virtuous trait of 'tam,' wholesomeness, simplicity.

Judaism believes that while God is capable of making anything happen, it is forbidden to rely on miracles. The Talmud teaches that if a person is in a situation or place that seems completely hopeless, if he has the ability to distance himself from the situation but chooses not to, he can pray all he wants but God does not listen to his prayers. God expects him to move.[93]

This is not to say that life is not complicated. Life presents us with difficult decisions that require careful consideration. Simplicity, purity, should not be confused with the bliss of willful ignorance. On the contrary, that is laziness.

The attainment of true simplicity requires patience and hard work. It requires brutal honesty, and suppression of the ego to get to the heart of a matter and understand it at its simplest elements.

This is what the Torah means when it affords to the rare individual the superlative appellation, "tam". Pure. And this is what the Torah means when it commands each of us to be "pure with the Lord your God."[94]

Because of our two-pronged approach to business ownership and because of the limitations of conventional accounting, consolidated reported earnings may reveal relatively little about our true economic performance. Charlie and I, both as owners and managers, virtually ignore such consolidated numbers. However, we will also report to you the earnings of each major business we control, numbers we consider of great importance. These figures, along with other information we will supply about the individual businesses, should generally aid you in making judgments about them.

Owner's Manual, Fifth Principle

With all your possessions acquire insight.

Proverbs 4:7

For My thoughts are not your thoughts.

Isaiah 55:8

Do not look at the container, but at what it contains, for a new flask may contain old wine, and an old flask may not contain anything, even new wine.

Rabbi Meir[95]

5

Insight

While visiting New York City, Warren Buffett sat down in a movie theatre in Times Square. The year was 1965 and the movie was Disney's latest blockbuster, Mary Poppins. Inspired by the movie, he and his partner Charlie Munger took their families to Disneyland in California that summer. They were not there to enjoy the rides. They were doing research.

While visiting New York City, Warren Buffett sat down in a movie theatre in Times Square. The year was 1965 and the movie was Disney's latest blockbuster, Mary Poppins. Inspired by the movie, he and his partner Charlie Munger took their families to Disneyland in California that summer. They were not there to enjoy the rides. They were doing research.

Later that year, Warren Buffett met with Walt Disney and was impressed with Disney's focus, enthusiasm, and love of his work. Disney, who had never heard of the thirty-five year old investor from Omaha, gave Warren Buffett a private tour of the park, including a peek at the newest attraction, The Pirates of the Caribbean Ride, which cost the company $17 million.

The Disney company was valued at $80 million. Soon after his visit, Warren Buffett purchased a 5% stake in the Disney company for $4 million. Today Disney is an enterprise valued at almost $200 billion.

At the time of Warren Buffett's investment, the market valued Disney at $80 million based on its theme park and movie businesses. Wall Street deliberately overlooked the fact that Mary Poppins by itself had brought in $30 million in earnings that year, reasoning, "Mary Poppins is great this year, but you are not going to have another Mary Poppins next year so their reported earnings will be down."

Warren Buffett saw things differently. He understood that Disney could re-release Mary Poppins to an audience of new kids seven years later, and they could charge more.

At the time, Disney had a library of over 200 movies, including box office sensations such as Bambi, Snow White, and Cinderella. The market completely ignored their value.

"They wrote them all down to zero – there were no residual values placed on the value of any Disney picture up through the '60s."[96]

Warren Buffett's investment in Disney demonstrates his fifth principle; develop the ability to sift through numbers and data in order to identify what really matters and what does not.

> *"There is a difference between what is measurable and what is meaningful."*

Understanding this important difference requires insight.

Annual reports can be filled with all sorts of large and impressive statistics and figures that are factually true, but sometimes completely irrelevant to the value of the company. About these Warren Buffett applies the saying,

> *"A horse that can count to ten is a remarkable horse but not a remarkable mathematician."*[97]

The Talmudic sage Rabbi Yannai said, "Be a tail to lions, rather than head to foxes."[98] Being the head is not always valuable. It depends on what you are the head of.
Warren Buffett echoes this saying exactly.

> *"At Berkshire, we much prefer owning a non–controlling but substantial portion of a wonderful company to owning 100% of a so–so business; it's better to have a partial interest in the Hope diamond than to own all of a rhinestone."*[99]

A low purchase price does not always indicate a bargain. When purchasing a business he says,

> *"Better a good business purchased at a fair price than a fair business at a bargain price."*[100]

Applying insight to identify relevant numbers on a spreadsheet is one thing. Real life is not always so readily neat and tidy. The important factors that measure true value are usually less concrete, and tend to fly under most people's radars. The more ephemeral qualities require genuine insight to recognize.

Insight | 63

Coke for example, has a strong intrinsic value based on its brand recognition. Warren Buffett once said, "If you gave me $100 billion and said, 'Take away the soft-drink leadership of Coca-Cola in the world,' I'd give it back to you and say it can't be done."[101]

Benjamin Graham was very conservative and generally focused on investments with a margin of safety based on tangible assets and annual earnings. Warren Buffett took Graham's philosophy to another level.

He saw other meaningful qualities that were not reflected in the company's book value alone. After factoring in these meaningful, though not easily measurable, qualities Warren Buffett determines to himself what he believes to be the company's real intrinsic value.

This concept is best illustrated in a Biblical story about the prophet Samuel. God sent Samuel to anoint a new king over Israel. Samuel traveled to Bethlehem to the home of a man named Jesse who had seven sons. When he arrived he saw Jesse's eldest son, Eliab, handsome and tall, standing before him. Samuel thought to himself, "Surely he is the one that God wants me to anoint as king."

But God said to Samuel, "Pay no attention to his appearance or his stature, for I have rejected him. For not as man sees [does God see]; man sees only what is visible, but God sees into the heart."[102]

A central principle in Judaism is to emulate God. Just as He is kind, you must be kind. Just as He is merciful, you must be merciful.[103] And just as he is able to look past what is measurable to see what is meaningful, you can do that as well. To do so requires insight.

> "You can gain some insight into the differences between book value and intrinsic value by looking at one form of investment, a college education. Think of the education's cost as its 'book value.' If this cost is to be accurate, it should include the earnings that were foregone by the student because he chose college rather than a job.
>
> For this exercise, we will ignore the important non-economic benefits of an education and focus strictly on its economic value. First, we must estimate the earnings that the graduate will receive over his lifetime and subtract from that figure an estimate of what he would have earned had he lacked his education. That gives us an excess earnings figure, which must then be discounted, at an appropriate interest rate, back to graduation day. The dollar result equals the intrinsic economic value of the education.
>
> Some graduates will find that the book value of their education exceeds its intrinsic value, which means that whoever paid for the education didn't get his money's worth. In other cases, the intrinsic value of an education will far exceed its book value, a result that proves capital was wisely deployed. In all cases, what is clear is that book value is meaningless as an indicator of intrinsic value."[104]

When others talk to you, insight means listening carefully and detecting seemingly insignificant subtleties in their words that may have significant, sometimes critical, implications.

Warren Buffett tells a story about a man who comes to town and sees an old man with a mean-looking German shepherd.

> 'He looked at the dog a little tentatively and he said, 'Does your dog bite?' The old-timer said, 'Nope.' So the stranger

> *reached down to pet him and the dog lunged at him and practically took off his arm, and the stranger…said, 'I thought you said your dog doesn't bite.' The guy answered, "This isn't my dog."*[105]

He tells a longer version of the same story about Ike Freidman, the manager of the Berkshire owned jewelry store, Borsheims.

> *"A story will illustrate why I enjoy Ike so much: Every two years I'm part of an informal group that gathers to have fun and explore a few subjects. Last September, meeting at Bishop's Lodge in Santa Fe, we asked Ike, his wife Roz, and his son Alan to come by and educate us on jewels and the jewelry business.*
>
> *Ike decided to dazzle the group, so he brought from Omaha about $20 million of particularly fancy merchandise. I was somewhat apprehensive – Bishop's Lodge is no Fort Knox – and I mentioned my concern to Ike at our opening party the evening before his presentation. Ike took me aside. 'See that safe?' he said. 'This afternoon we changed the combination and now even the hotel management doesn't know what it is.' I breathed easier. Ike went on: 'See those two big fellows with guns on their hips? They'll be guarding the safe all night.' I now was ready to rejoin the party. But Ike leaned closer: 'And besides, Warren,' he confided, 'the jewels aren't in the safe.*[106]

In the 19th century there was a brilliant rabbi named Rabbi Chaim of Brisk. One of the greatest Talmudists of his time, he was known for his unique method of analyzing Talmudic texts. One year, before the Passover holiday, a man approached Rabbi Chaim while he was teaching his students and asked Rabbi Chaim a question regarding a Passover seder ritual.

"Hypothetically," asked the man, "if someone does not have wine to fill the ceremonial cups, could he fulfill his ritual obligation at the seder by drinking four cups of milk?"

The students were eager to hear Rabbi Chaim use his brilliant command of texts and logic to construct an argument to answer the question.

They were disappointed when Rabbi Chaim offered no answer and instead immediately escorted the man out of the study hall. The students noticed that as he saw the man to the door, Rabbi Chaim discreetly reached into his own pocket, took out what appeared to be a substantial sum of money, and handed it to the man who asked the question. The man thanked Rabbi Chaim and went on his way.

When he returned to the students, they informed him that they had witnessed what transpired. It occurred to them after the fact that the Rabbi was sensitive enough to understand that the man was not really asking a theoretical question, but that he was lacking money to purchase wine. The question was not a question in Talmudic logic. It was a cry for help.

However, one thing still confused them. It seemed that the Rabbi gave the man a far greater sum of money than was required to purchase wine. Why so much?

To which the Rabbi answered, "As you know, there is a prohibition against eating milk together with meat. When he asked if he could use milk at the seder, I inferred not only that he lacked money for wine, but he also lacked money for meat to celebrate the holiday. So I gave him enough money to purchase both."

Just as Rabbi Chaim used his keen insight to identify the true meaning behind the man's question, insight should also be used to identify who is a true sage.

In Judaism a true sage is not measured strictly by how much information a scholar knows.

There is a tale of a secular professor of ethics, a man regarded as a great scholar, who was caught having an extramarital affair. He was subsequently asked whether he thought it an oxymoron to be an unethical professor of ethics. To which he answered, "You would not expect a teacher of geometry to be a triangle, would you? Then you should not expect a teacher of ethics to be ethical."

Judaism has a very different concept when it comes to identifying a true scholar.

The Talmud extols the virtues of the wise only if their wisdom is manifest in good deeds.[107]

A story is related about a renowned scholar who could recite the voluminous corpus of sacred literature by heart. He was also known to be of poor moral character. Upon his death the community came to the saintly Rabbi Nachman and requested that Rabbi Nachman honor the deceased by delivering a eulogy. To which Rabbi Nachman asked, "What should I say, 'Here lies a bag of books'?"[108]

Knowledge is not the sole criteria of being a true sage.

As Irving Bunim wrote in his book *Ethics From Sinai*, "Knowledge [is] only a means to an end. If a person's [knowledge] is greater than his deeds, and he does not translate it into blueprints and guidelines for actual behavior, he may be compared to someone who invents a complicated machine with wheels that turn and cogs that mesh, but which goes nowhere and does nothing. Surely such a device comes from wasted effort and produces more wasted effort."[109]

Most important of all, insight should be applied when evaluating your own success.

An interviewer once asked Warren Buffett, "Why would you give so much money to charity?"

Warren Buffett answered, "I can only eat three meals a day, sleep in one bed, and drive one car. From a material standpoint I already had everything I could ever want forty years ago."[110]

The reporter, who lacked insight, was dumbfounded. "That's amazing!" He exclaimed. "You are the number one investor in the world and you don't care about money."

Warren Buffett explained to him, "I enjoy making money because when I do it shows that I have done well at what I do. But just having money doesn't mean anything."

After officiating at countless funerals over many years, the Chief Rabbi of Britain, Lord Jonathan Sacks, noticed a pattern. "When people would speak about their deceased loved ones they praised them for being a devoted spouse, a loving parent, and a loyal friend. They were remembered for being charitable with their money and with their time, and for shouldering the responsibilities of the community."

No one ever spoke about the amount of money they had or the material possessions that they had accumulated. At the end we realize, "the things we spend most of our time pursuing turn out to be curiously irrelevant when it comes to seeing the value of a life as a whole."[111]

Warren Buffett expresses the exact sentiments.

"I would say that when you get to be my age or a little younger - I'm eighty-two - if people that you want to have love you, love you, you're a success. You can have all the money in the world. You can have buildings named after you, hospital wings, whatever, and unless you have people that really care about you, you're not a success."[112]

Money is measurable, but the insightful person knows that real value and real success in life is found in metrics that are not always easily measurable, but are infinitely meaningful.

Accounting consequences do not influence our operating or capital-allocation decisions. When acquisition costs are similar, we much prefer to purchase $2 of earnings that is not reportable by us under standard accounting principles than to purchase $1 of earnings that is reportable. This is precisely the choice that often faces us since entire businesses (whose earnings will be fully reportable) frequently sell for double the pro-rata price of small portions (whose earnings will be largely unreportable). In aggregate and over time, we expect the unreported earnings to be fully reflected in our intrinsic business value through capital gains.

Owner's Manual, Sixth Principle

The commerce of [wisdom] is better than the commerce of silver, and its gain is better than fine gold.

Proverbs 3:14

Precious treasure and oil are in the dwelling of the wise man, but man's foolishness will swallow it up.

Proverbs 21:20

A woman of valor who can find? Her price is beyond pearls.

Proverbs 31:10

6
Wisdom

In the 1960s American Express had a subsidiary program called field warehousing. For a fee, Amex dispatched investigators to inspect a company's warehouse and, upon verification, Amex would provide receipts vouching for the existence and value of certain commodities. The client business could then take those receipts to a bank and use them as collateral to borrow money.

One of Amex's biggest clients for this program was Anthony "Tino" De Angelis, known at that time as the Salad Oil King. Tino had built his salad oil kingdom by capitalizing on a law passed by president John F. Kennedy called the Food for Peace Act. Through his company, Allied Crude Vegetable Oil, Tino took advantage of government subsidies to purchase from farmers surplus soybean oil at low prices to be sold overseas, for a profit, to distressed countries.

In September of 1963 rumors were circulating that Russia had a failed soybean crop and would soon be looking to purchase large quantities of soybean oil from the United States. If true, the price of soybean oil would skyrocket. Tino got greedy. Through the field warehousing program, he hired Amex to write him receipts for massive quantities of soybean oil stored at his warehouse in Bayonne, New Jersey. Then he borrowed money from multiple banks against those receipts to purchase futures contracts on soybean oil. Tino went all in, betting the house that the price of oil would rise and that he would make a fortune from his contracts and from his own oil reserves.

But the rumors proved false and the soybean oil market crashed. Overnight his futures contracts became worthless and Tino could not meet his margin call. When his creditors came to the warehouse in Bayonne, New Jersey to seize their salad oil to cover the debts, they opened the tanks and were shocked to discover that they had been scammed! Instead of the precious salad oil, the tanks were filled with mostly worthless seawater.

The aftermath of this episode was one of the most traumatic market scandals in history and came to be known as the Great Salad Oil Swindle.

For years Tino had been taking advantage of American Express's lax inspections and using them to vouch for hundreds of millions of pounds of non-existent oil. Like a magician, Tino used a variety of different tricks and illusions to create salad oil out of thin air.

After an inspector checked a tank of oil, Tino would quickly drain the tank using a system of underground pipes. As the inspector walked through the warehouse, the oil would be shuttled to fill a nearby empty tank just in time for the inspector to check and find it full with the oil that had already been accounted for.

Other times he would confuse the inspectors by walking them through a maze of tanks. All the while his employees would change the numbers on tanks so that the disoriented inspectors would inspect the same tank multiple times.

The most obvious trick of all was a thin layer of oil floating on a tank full of water so that all that an inspector would see from the top was oil.

At the time of the margin call Tino had receipts outstanding for a quantity of soybean oil greater than all of the soybean oil in the United States as reported by the U.S. Department of Agriculture. He had borrowed money on 1.8 billion pounds of oil while his warehouse could only hold 500 million pounds at full capacity.

The losses to creditors were devastating. $175 million spread out over fifty different lending institutions, each with hundreds of customers. The worst pessimists feared that the losses coupled with the blow to investor confidence could bring down the entire stock market. Someone needed to take responsibility. But who?

It was certainly not going to be Tino. Tino was completely broke and immediately filed for bankruptcy.

The creditors' next look was to American Express. The only reason the banks had lent money to Tino in the first place was because Amex had vouched for his oil. Amex, they thought, should be liable to pay. The problem for the creditors was that the warehouse program was a subsidiary of Amex which legally was a separate entity from American Express - for exactly this reason, to protect the parent company. The warehouse program subsidiary declared bankruptcy which technically absolved Amex from any liability.

American Express CEO Howard Clark released a statement saying that American Express was not legally obligated to the creditors; however, he added "American Express feels morally bound to do everything that it can to see that such excess liabilities are satisfied." When he made this statement, he did so recognizing that there was a chance that the debts amounted to more money than Amex had.

The creditors breathed a sigh of relief.

American Express shareholders were furious. After Clark's announcement the stock plummeted from $60 a share and eventually fell as low as $35 a share. From the shareholders perspective Clark was foolish to waste their money to fulfill what they considered to be some frivolous virtue. Amex was a business not a charity! If the law said they were not responsible then they were not responsible! The shareholders formally contested his decision and filed a lawsuit against Amex.

Where everyone else saw foolishness, Warren Buffett saw wisdom. He flew out to New York and paid a personal visit to Howard Clark. He applauded Clark for doing the right thing. He volunteered to testify in court on Amex's behalf where he told shareholders that they should be congratulating Clark for putting the matter behind them. They should view the settlement paid out as a dividend check that was lost in the mail.

Finally Warren Buffett put his money where his mouth was. He took 40% of his own available capital and he purchased a 5% interest in American Express.

He reasoned as follows. American Express' main businesses were traveler's checks and charge cards. These products are only as good as the reputation of the company that backs them. Warren Buffett observed that even after the scandal vendors and merchants continued to accept American Express as readily as money. The name and reputation that Amex had established since the company's founding in 1850 was still considered by the general public to be a good name.

Before the scandal Amex was in possession of large reserves of salad oil that had a definite and easily calculable market value. Post scandal, they had nothing but their good name.

The market preferred good oil to a good name, but thousands of years prior, King Solomon wrote in the book of Ecclesiastes, "A good name is better than good oil."[113]

Warren Buffett opted for the Wisdom of Solomon, and over the next ten years it proved to be the right choice. His investment in Amex increased tenfold.

The previous chapter spoke about finding hidden value by adding the meaningful to the measurable. That takes insight. There are other times when we are forced to choose, to sacrifice, to forego the measurable in order to attain the meaningful, to turn down a dollar now for two dollars later. Those choices are never easy, they sometimes require great courage, and they always require wisdom.

When a young Solomon first became King of Israel, God came to Solomon in a dream and offered to grant Solomon a wish. Solomon could have asked for long life, riches, or victory over his enemies. Instead he asked "for a heart of wisdom to judge the people and discern good from evil."[114]

The Talmud compares the story of Solomon's request for wisdom to a king who wished to reward his favorite officer by granting the officer any request. The officer realized that any riches or honors that the king could give to him may only be temporary.

So he decided to ask for the hand of the king's daughter in marriage, as that would encompass and guarantee everything.[115]

The Talmud sites an ancient proverb, "He who has wisdom has everything. He who lacks wisdom has nothing."[116]

Wisdom means recognizing that sometimes, as the Talmud says, there is a short road which is really the long road, and there is a long road which is really the short road.[117] Cutting corners or taking the easy way out, ethically or otherwise, seems like the way to success, but a person with wisdom sees the bigger picture.

The Talmudic sage Rabbi Shimon Ben Elazar taught that when the youth tell you to build and the elders tell you to tear down, listen to the elders. Whereas the building of the inexperienced youth can lead to destruction, the apparent destruction recommended by the elders is really a form of building.

The paradigmatic example that illustrates this principle is the story of Solomon's son, Rechavam. After the death of his father Solomon, the nation gathered and requested that, as the newly appointed king, Rechavam should lower the taxes. Before addressing the people, Rechavam consulted with two groups of advisors; the first group consisted of the elders who had advised his father Solomon, and the second set of advisors were Rechavam's young and inexperienced peers. The elders advised him to give in to the demands of the people. Lower the taxes today and you will be able to build their trust. His peers had a different plan. They advised the king to come down on the people with a heavy hand. Raise the taxes just to show them that you're the boss. Rechavam adopted the policy of the young over the old. He raised the taxes and as a result there was a revolt followed by a great schism that caused Rechavam to lose half of his Kingdom.[118]

Wisdom is also required when weighing which attributes are the most meaningful.

Warren Buffett learned from the Omaha developer Peter Kiewit to look for certain attributes when hiring people. Kiewit warned, though, not to sacrifice the attributes that are the most essential.

> *"He looked for three things in hiring people: integrity, intelligence, and energy. And if the person didn't have the first two, then the latter two would kill him. Because if they don't have integrity, you don't want them to be smart and energetic, you want them to be dumb and lazy."*[19]

The Talmud teaches the exact same lesson in a parable about a man who instructed his agent to move a supply of wheat up to a loft for storage. The employee carried out his instructions, and when he reported back, his boss asked him, "Did you remember to mix in a preservative?" "No." replied the employee. To which the employer replied, "Then it were better that you had not carried it up at all."[120]

When Warren Buffett speaks to students he instructs them to use wisdom when choosing a career.

"When it comes to choosing between something lucrative but not personally meaningful, or something personally meaningful but less lucrative, I never met anyone who chose meaningful and regretted it."[121]

The Talmudic sage Rabbi Yossi Ben Kisma tells a story.

"Once I was walking along the road when a man met me and greeted me. He said to me, 'Rabbi, where do you come from?' I replied, 'I come from a great city of sages and scholars.' He said to me, 'Rabbi, if you are willing to live with us in our place, I will give you a million gold dinars, as well as precious stones and pearls.' I replied, 'Were you to give me all the silver and gold and precious stones and pearls in the world, I would not live anywhere except in a place of Torah.'"[122]

The Talmudic sage Hillel teaches that a person who acquires a good name does so for himself.[123] The commentator known as Rabbi Yonah Gerondi wrote that when a person dies, his physical assets transfer over to others. Everything that a person earns in life will eventually end up in the hands of someone else, except for a good name. A good name is a non-transferable asset that cannot be bequeathed or inherited. The only one who ultimately profits from a good name is the person who earned it.

Warren Buffett has been investing his whole life. He is well aware that he won't be able to take his money with him when he passes. With wisdom he has recognized that his most important investment all along has been in his good name. And it will be his good name that will endure as his most valuable and valued asset.

We use debt sparingly and, when we do borrow, we attempt to structure our loans on a long-term fixed-rate basis. We will reject interesting opportunities rather than over-leverage our balance sheet. This conservatism has penalized our results but it is the only behavior that leaves us comfortable, considering our fiduciary obligations to policyholders, lenders and the many equity holders who have committed unusually large portions of their net worth to our care. (As one of the Indianapolis "500" winners said: "To finish first, you must first finish.")

Owner's Manual, Seventh Principle

"If you do not have what to pay, why should he take your bed from under you?"

Proverbs 22:27

Better that you do not vow at all than that you vow and not pay.

Ecclesiastes 5:4

A person must contemplate and survey this actions and his conduct to see whether they are good or not, so as not to risk the loss of his soul.

Rabbi Moses Chaim Luzzatto[124]

7

Caution

On April 13, 1993 Don Calhoun, a $5 an hour office supply salesman, became a millionaire. During halftime at a Chicago Bulls basketball game, Calhoun participated in a promotional contest sponsored by Coca-Cola and Lettuce Entertain You Enterprises. One fan, chosen randomly from over 18,000 people, was given a chance to win a million dollars. All he had to do was sink a basket from the opposite free throw line, seventy feet away.

The odds of hitting a shot like that were considered to be nearly impossible, less than one in a million.

Before the contest, Lettuce Entertain You approached National Indemnity, one of Warren Buffett's many insurance companies, and asked for a quote on an insurance policy to cover the contest in the unlikely event that a contestant would win the prize. The case landed in the lap of one of National Indemnity's actuaries. There are no actuary tables that have predetermined odds for seventy foot basketball shots. As it happened, this particular actuary was himself a basketball player and for many years he coached at the Jewish

Community Center in Omaha. To do some research for this assignment, he took his team of eight actuaries down to the JCC gym and he gave each of them ten chances at the seventy foot shot.

They were all astounded to find that of the eighty total shots attempted, four went in. Five percent. If their small sample set of actuaries was representative of the general population, exact odds on a million dollar bet would be a premium of $50,000.

Insurance companies don't make money by offering clients policies with exact odds. He called back Lettuce Entertain You and gave them a quote for coverage based on his experiment plus a margin of safety.

Lettuce Entertain You thought the quote was excessive. They were not expecting to pay tens of thousands of dollars to cover what they thought was a highly improbable, if not impossible, feat. They decided to shop around, and they found Hole in One Insurance Company eager to cover the bet for a price significantly cheaper than the price offered by National Indemnity. Hole in One specialized in covering sporting contests with sensational prize giveaways that they believed to be unwinnable. Someone forgot to tell Don Calhoun this contest was unwinnable. In front of thousands of fans he sent the basketball sailing through the air across the court directly through the rim, the ball hit nothing but net.

His prize was paid in twenty annual installments of $50,000.

Hole in One never disclosed how much they charged for the policy, but it was nowhere near the hefty sum National Indemnity quoted. They told reporters that it was "in the thousands." If their past history is any indication, they had previously insured a golf tournament hole-in-one million dollar give away for as little as $1,200.

National indemnity avoided a catastrophic loss by applying Warren Buffett's seventh principle, caution.

That is not to say that Warren Buffett's insurance companies don't write unusual policies.

> "We insured: (1) The life of Mike Tyson for a sum that is large initially and that, fight-by-fight, gradually declines to zero over the next few years; (2) Lloyd's against more than 225 of its 'names' dying during the year; and (3) The launch, and a year of orbit, of two Chinese satellites. Happily, satellites are orbiting, the Lloyd's folk avoided abnormal mortality, and if Mike Tyson looked any healthier, no one would get in the ring with him."[125]

In 2014 they insured a billion dollar prize offered by Quicken Loans to anyone who could predict with 100% accuracy the outcome of the NCAA March Madness Basketball tournament.

The chances of predicting the outcome of all sixty-three games is less than one in nine quintillion.

That's 9,000,000,000,000,000,000.

When his insurance companies take on risk, they do so in a responsible way, exercising the attribute of caution.

Geico insurance, another insurance company owned by Berkshire Hathaway, is another example. In times when there were price wars and competitors were offering outrageously low premiums, Geico preferred to write fewer policies rather than offer policies at prices below their comfort level. When reckless insurance companies suffer catastrophic losses they are forced to declare bankruptcy, leaving customers with unpaid claims.

When hurricane Sandy ravaged New York in 2012, GEICO had to pay out claims to 46,906 owners of damaged cars, the largest single loss in the company's long history, and they still turned a profit on the year.[126]

A cheap promise from an insolvent insurance company is really no promise at all. Or in Warren Buffett's words, "to finish first you must finish."[127]

Warren Buffett provides guidelines for his principle of caution.

> "At bottom, a sound insurance operation needs to adhere to four disciplines. It must (1) understand all exposures that might cause a policy to incur losses; (2) conservatively assess the likelihood of any exposure actually causing a loss and the probable cost if it does; (3) set a premium that, on average, will deliver a profit after both prospective loss costs and operating expenses are covered; and (4) be willing to walk away if the appropriate premium can't be obtained. Many insurers pass the first three tests and flunk the fourth. They simply can't turn their back on business that is being eagerly written by their competitors. That old line, 'The other guy is doing it, so we must as well,' spells trouble in any business, but in none more so than insurance."[128]

Judaism puts a very high premium on the attribute of caution. Warren Buffett's principles echo the warning of our sages when it comes to avoiding catastrophic spiritual losses caused by sinning.

Rabbi Moses Chaim Luzzatto, in his classic work of ethics, *The Path of the Just*, writes that a person must first ponder what constitutes true good that will bring reward, and what constitutes true evil that will cause punishment. Once that assessment is made, a person should not perform any deed without first weighing on the scales, and carefully considering the cost.

As it says in Proverbs, "The clever person saw wrongdoing and concealed himself, but the foolish person committed transgressions and was punished."[129] The wise person prepares his path to make sure there is no likelihood that he will come to sin. But the foolish person "feels secure, and when they fall it is without any prior knowledge of the obstacle that was in their way."[130]

On the Biblical verse, "Come to [the city of] Cheshbon"[131] the Talmud makes a play on words. Cheshbon was the name of an Emorite city, but the word Cheshbon can also mean a balance sheet. As if to say, at all times weigh the liability of a good deed against its profit, and the profit of a sin against its liability.[132] In modern Hebrew the word 'Cheshbon' means arithmetic, as if the sages of old were telling us, before you commit to an action, do the math.

Jack Ringwalt, the owner of National Indemnity put it this way, "There is no such thing as a bad risk. There are only bad rates."[133]

On a golf outing with a group of friends, GEICO chairman Jack Byrne said that in exchange for an $11 premium paid in advance he would give $10,000 to anyone who hit a hole-in-one over the weekend. Everyone present paid the premium except for Warren Buffett. Based on a self-assessment of his golfing skills he evaluated the $11 premium as too expensive.[134]

The author of the Mishnah, Rabbi Yehudah the Nasi, taught that you should "be as cautious with a minor sin as you are with a major one."[135] Stated differently, there are no minor sins. Certainly there are some crimes that are worse than others –

murder is worse than stealing. And there are different degrees within the same sin – stealing a car is worse than stealing a candy bar. But that does not mean that you should be any less meticulous or cautious when weighing your actions relating to so called minor sins, because every sin should be viewed as major. Before engaging in a so-called victimless crime, you must exercise the same caution that you would use before engaging in a sin against another person. Because there are no victimless crimes, at the very least by committing such actions you harm yourself.

Often the price of a sin in the long run is far higher than the small benefit you receive. Warren Buffett values a good night's sleep over taking risk for the potential of slightly higher profits.

Health Guru Harvey Diamond notes how we sometimes put certain kinds of food into our mouths that are so harmful to so many parts of our body for the sole reason that they provide momentary pleasure to a few microscopic dots on our tongue.

When you sin you cause irreparable damage to others and to yourself for a fleeting pleasure that is gone in an instant.

Conversely, when you resist the urge to sin you lose a moment of pleasure but forever look back with pride that you were able to demonstrate restraint and discipline in the face of temptation.

The Talmudic sage Rabbi Yehudah taught that in the end of days every man will see his evil inclination personified and slaughtered before him. The wicked will see that his temptation was the size of a thread, and the righteous will see that his was the size of a mountain. The wicked will cry when he realizes how easy it would have been to overcome his momentary vices, and the righteous will cry tears of joy when he celebrates the achievements he accomplished.[136]

"Fortunate is the one who is always cautious."[137] Because when you do the math, you see that sin never pays.

A managerial "wish list" will not be filled at shareholder expense. We will not diversify by purchasing entire businesses at control prices that ignore long-term economic consequences to our shareholders. We will only do with your money what we would do with our own, weighing fully the values you can obtain by diversifying your own portfolios through direct purchases in the stock market.

Owner's Manual, Eighth Principle

Take from it every man according to what he can eat.

Exodus 16:16

There is one who acts rich but has nothing, and one who feigns poverty but has great wealth.

Proverbs 13:8

Thehbvgb righteous eats to sate his appetite, but the stomach of the wicked shall feel want.

Proverbs 13:25

8

Frugality

On September 6, 2007 the city of Omaha woke up to a breaking news update. There had been an attempted break-in at 5505 Farnam Street, home of Omaha's most famous citizen, Warren Buffett. We anxiously sat next to the radio listening to newscasters speculate as the story unfolded. Was it an attempted assassination? A case of industrial espionage? A deranged stalker? It turned out to be none of the above.

In the summer of 2007 there had been a series of break-ins and petty thefts in the Dundee area in Omaha where Warren Buffett lives. The break-ins were smash and grab jobs targeting ladies purses. The Dundee area is a nice, but modest, ungated neighborhood.

The man who tried to break into Warren Buffett's house was just a run-of-the-mill petty thief hoping to snatch a purse. He had no idea that the house belonged to one of the richest men in the world. At 10 p.m., he walked up to Warren Buffett's front door wearing a ski mask, a dark cap, and holding a toy gun, and he rang the doorbell. He was seen through the security camera, and was stopped by one of Warren Buffett's private security guards.

Warren Buffett lives in the same house that he bought in 1958 for $31,500. From the outside the house does not look much different from any of the houses in the area.

This was simply a case of the unluckiest burglar in history.

Warren Buffett is known for his simple life. He lives in a modest house and drives a modest car. He does not own a yacht, and only started flying in a private plane when he was convinced that it was more cost effective and efficient for his company, given the amount of traveling that he does. Even so, he named his first private jet, "The Indefensible," out of contrition for earlier criticism for corporate CEOs that partook in such "indefensible" luxuries like private jets.

There is no doubt that much of Warren Buffett's frugal nature is attributed to the principle expressed by the Talmudic sage ben Zoma. "Who is wealthy?" He asked, "The one who is happy with his lot."[138]

When asked about his seemingly minimalist lifestyle relative to his wealth, Warren Buffett points out, "I can only eat three meals a day, drive one car, live in so many rooms."[139]

Who defines our needs? Sometimes when people achieve affluence and prominence they become cognizant of certain "needs" that they never felt were necessary before. They need to live in a bigger house, they need to live in a fancier neighborhood, they need to drive a more luxurious car, and they need to wear more expensive clothes. They experience new social pressures to fulfil these needs. When people give into these pressures they are allowing others to define their needs for them. The frugal person determines for himself what his needs are. He does not feel compelled to alter his lifestyle based on what others may think.

There is more to Warren Buffett's frugality than just contentment.

Washington Post CEO Katherine Graham told a story about a time that she and Warren Buffett were traveling together. She needed to make a call at a pay phone and, not having any change on her, she asked Warren Buffett if he had a dime. Warren Buffett fished into his pocket, but only came up with a quarter. Payphones did not give change so, not wanting to give an extra fifteen cents to the phone company, Warren Buffett started looking for a store that would give him change for a quarter.[140]

While this seems extreme, in principle it makes perfect sense. There is no shame in exerting a little extra effort, or experiencing minor inconveniences to save some money. That is frugality.

Warren Buffett's ninth principle stresses that this is all the more important when the money in question belongs to someone else.

One of the early fixed principles of what Charlie Munger calls "The Berkshire System" is: "There would be almost nothing at conglomerate headquarters except a tiny office suite containing a Chairman, a CFO, and a few assistants who mostly helped the CFO with auditing, internal control, etc."[141]

In his annual letter Warren Buffett boasts about the small staff working in the Berkshire Hathaway corporate headquarters in Omaha.

Some would call this behavior cheap, but frugal should not be confused with cheap.

When Jacob, the Biblical patriarch, was about to encounter his brother Esau, Jacob prepared for battle. He crossed over a river, arranged his camp in a military formation, and prepared his servants and his sons for a possible altercation with Esau and his 400 men. Then "[Jacob] went back [across the river] by himself and there he wrestled with a [mysterious] man until the break of dawn."[142]

This was the famous episode of Jacob wrestling with an angel.

The sages of the Talmud were puzzled. Why did Jacob leave the safety of his camp and cross back over the river alone? What was so important on the other side of the river that was worth risking his life for? The Talmudic sage Rabbi Elazar answers that he went back to retrieve certain small containers that he had left behind. While this may seem foolish, stingy, perhaps even greedy, the sages learned from this a valuable lesson. The truly righteous value their money.[143]

Judaism does not scorn wealth. On the contrary, money earned honestly represents hard work. To waste money demonstrates a lack of respect for money, which in turn signifies a lack of respect for honest hard work.

While all charitable giving should be commended and encouraged, the great Jewish philosopher Maimonides teaches that not all giving is equal. Two people can give identical gifts, but one act of charity can be considered more virtuous than the other depending on the attitude of the giver.

I heard a story from a fundraiser for a charitable institution who visited a successful and generous business owner for a solicitation. The meeting was a success, and the philanthropist wrote a big check to the institution. After the meeting the business owner offered to accompany the fundraiser on his way to his next appointment. As they walked outside his office building in New York City, the business owner offered to treat the fundraiser to a soft drink from one of the street vendors. The fundraiser agreed and as they approached the first available vendor, the business owner said, "Not here. I usually buy from the man down the street, his prices are five cents cheaper."

The fundraiser was flabbergasted. He asked in astonishment, "You would walk out of your way to save a nickel?"

"Yes," answered the business owner. "And I am happy you see that. I want you to know that I value my money. I don't part with money easily. I donate to your organization because I believe in the good work that you do."

In his autobiography, Benjamin Franklin defined frugality, "Make no expense but to do good to others or yourself; i.e., waste nothing."[144]

Having billions of dollars does not make the value of those dollars any lower. Every cent can be used to do good to yourself, and if all of your needs are met, to do good to others.

To date Warren Buffett has never paid shareholders a dividend, but he views every dollar earned by Berkshire as belonging to the shareholders. His job is to do the best that he can with the money that was entrusted in his care.

> *"If we can't do better than you with your money we will give it to you as a dividend and let you do better with it."*

In his ninth principle of investing, Warren Buffett invokes the Biblical principle, "Love your neighbor as you love yourself."[145]

The verse implies that before a person can love another person, he must love himself. If a person is lacking in love or respect for himself or for his own property, then he is not capable of truly showing love towards others or towards their property.

There is a golden mean between stinginess on the one hand and generosity on the other. Both extremes demonstrate a lack of respect for money.

The overly generous, as mentioned above, *under*value their money. Those who undervalue their own money will naturally undervalue the money of others. When you see a CEO frivolously spending fortunes of money on his own extravagant personal lifestyle it should raise red flags in the minds of shareholders and indicate how he might spend their money.

The overly stingy *over*value their money.

Irving Bunim, in *Ethics from Sinai*, tells a story about a Rabbi who saw a rich man eating poor man's food, black bread and radishes. He recommended that the man upgrade his diet to fancier foods. The Rabbi's students asked him why he made such a prescription. To which the Rabbi answered, "If this is the way that he treats himself, how do you think he will treat the poor?"[146]

A verse in Proverbs states, "A man who is kind to himself is a man of kindness."[147]

While human life is valued above all, that does not mean that we do not show respect for property, even inanimate objects.

When Moses turned the Nile River to blood in Egypt, he instructed his brother Aaron to carry out the plague by striking the Nile. The Talmudic sage, Rabbi Tanhum, asks why Moses did not perform the act himself. The answer given is that Moses felt gratitude to the Nile. When Pharaoh decreed that all Jewish baby boys should be killed, Moses's mother saved Moses' life by placing him in a basket and sending him floating down the Nile. The Nile was an inanimate object, and yet Moses viewed it as having taken part in saving his life, so he showed the Nile his appreciation. From this we can only imagine how much appreciation Moses had for his courageous mother.[148]

The sages learn from this that a person should show respect even to inanimate objects, for if we do so, how much more so will we come to respect people.

Buffett says,

> "We regard the holder of one share of B stock as the equal of our large institutional investors"[149]

Just as he values every penny, he values all of his shareholders.

Judaism is not an aesthetic religion. We are encouraged to enjoy life. But when we spend on ourselves we must make sure that we receive value. Excessive purchasing of material objects to fulfil our desires will not make us happy, and will not provide true value. Celebrating happy occasions with family, spreading our happiness around with loved ones, and helping those in need are priceless luxuries well worth the cost.

We feel noble intentions should be checked periodically against results. We test the wisdom of retaining earnings by assessing whether retention, over time, delivers shareholders at least $1 of market value for each $1 retained. To date, this test has been met. We will continue to apply it on a five-year rolling basis. As our net worth grows, it is more difficult to use retained earnings wisely.

Owner's Manual, Ninth Principle

Now the man Moses was exceedingly humble, more than any person on the earth.

Numbers 12:3

He who loves rebuke loves knowledge, but he who hates reproof is a brute.

Proverbs 12:1

Humbly walks the duck, but its eyes are turned to heaven.

Bava Kama 92b

9
Humility

My grandfather worked in the diamond industry. He began as a diamond cutter in a factory, and eventually went out on his own and started his own wholesale diamond company. After my father graduated from college, like his father before him, he trained and worked as a cutter. After working for a large company for a number of years he left and joined my grandfather in his business.

As a young boy, I always imagined that I would join them someday. I remember the moment that changed.

I was about twelve years old and the extended family had gathered on a Sunday at my grandparent's home, as we often did. I was sitting on a couch in the den with my grandfather. He told me a story that forever changed the way that I looked at the family business, and taught me an important lesson about life.

In 1969 America was getting ready to send the first man to the moon. The country seemed in a frenzy of excitement. But on 47th street, the heart of New York City's diamond district, there was anxiety and even feelings of impending doom. The moon was unchartered territory. It was anybody's guess what the astronauts would find when they landed. What if they dug into the moon's surface and pulled out a shovel full of diamonds? The astronauts would fill up the shuttle with diamonds, and as the shuttle came plummeting back to earth the price of diamonds would fall in tandem. The market would be flooded with moon diamonds, and my grandfather's business, along with the rest of the industry, would be finished.

My grandfather's advice, "When you grow up, be an undertaker. There's no recession."

Warren Buffett has certain investments that he refers to as "inevitables."

> *"Companies such as Coca–Cola and Gillette might well be labeled 'The Inevitables.' Forecasters may differ a bit in their predictions of exactly how much soft drink or shaving-equipment business these companies will be doing in ten or twenty years...however, no sensible observer – not even these companies' most vigorous competitors, assuming they are assessing the matter honestly – questions that Coke and Gillette will dominate their fields worldwide for an investment lifetime. Indeed, their dominance will probably strengthen."*

The truth is, while some things may seem like they will never go out of style, Warren Buffett knows very well that nothing, even diamonds, lasts forever. There are no such things as true "inevitables."

The "inevitability" of the aforementioned companies is predicated on,

> *"The vital work that these companies must continue to carry out, in such areas as manufacturing, distribution, packaging and product innovation."*

Things can also go bad when companies lose their focus.

> *"A far more serious problem occurs when the management of a great company gets sidetracked and neglects its wonderful base business while purchasing other businesses that are so–so or worse. Unfortunately, that is precisely what transpired years ago at both Coke and Gillette. (Would you believe that a few decades back they were growing shrimp at Coke and exploring for oil at Gillette?) Loss of focus is what most worries Charlie and me when we contemplate investing in businesses that in general look outstanding. All too often, we've seen value stagnate in the presence of hubris or of boredom that caused the attention of managers to wander."*[150]

The Talmudic sage Hillel said, "Don't count on yourself until the day you die."[151] The obvious question is, how do you know when you are going to die? You don't, and that's the point. Today may be your last day, or you may live another hundred years. As long as you're alive you have to maintain focus.

To illustrate this point the Talmud tells the story of Yochanan Kohein Gadol. After a long life of establishing a reputation as a saintly and pious man, at the age of eighty years old he fell off the wagon and became a heretic.[152]

The hardest time to stay focused is when times are good. People have a tendency to coast and they attribute their success to their own efforts.

After a year of outstanding returns in 1997, Warren Buffett wrote to his shareholders,

> *"As tempting as it would be to declare victory, every investor can make money when stocks soar. One must avoid the error of the preening duck that quacks boastfully after a torrential rainstorm, thinking that its paddling skills have caused it to rise in the world."*[153]

The ninth principle states that nothing should be taken for granted. Everyone needs periodic evaluations to ensure that they are performing as they should, and no results are truly inevitable. Neglecting this principle leads to arrogance, but if you keep this principle in the front of your mind at all times it will lead to humility.

Warren Buffett says that mediocre is worse than bad. When you are in a bad situation you are aware that you need a change. But when circumstances are not bad, but not very good either, it is harder to make the decisions necessary to grow.

> *"My successor will need one other particular strength: the ability to fight off the ABCs of business decay, which are arrogance, bureaucracy and complacency. When these corporate cancers metastasize, even the strongest of companies can falter. The examples available to prove the point are legion, but to maintain friendships I will exhume only cases from the distant past.*
>
> *In their glory days, General Motors, IBM, Sears Roebuck and U.S. Steel sat atop huge industries. Their strengths seemed unassailable. But the destructive behavior I deplored above eventually led each of them to fall to depths that their CEOs*

and directors had not long before thought impossible. Their one-time financial strength and their historical earning power proved no defense."[154]

Complacency is when mediocre is accepted as adequate, and there is no drive to improve. Arrogance is having an exaggerated sense of your own abilities.

Warren Buffett perfectly defines arrogance in his coin flipping parable.

> *"I would like you to imagine a national coin-flipping contest. Let's assume we get 225 million Americans up tomorrow morning and we ask them all to wager a dollar. They go out in the morning at sunrise, and they all call the flip of a coin. If they call correctly, they win a dollar from those who called wrong. Each day the losers drop out, and on the subsequent day the stakes build as all previous winnings are put on the line. After ten flips on ten mornings, there will be approximately 220,000 people in the United States who have correctly called ten flips in a row. They each will have won a little over $1,000.*
>
> *Now this group will probably start getting a little puffed up about this, human nature being what it is. They may try to be modest, but at cocktail parties they will occasionally admit to attractive members of the opposite sex what their technique is, and what marvelous insights they bring to the field of flipping.*
>
> *Assuming that the winners are getting the appropriate rewards from the losers, in another ten days we will have 215 people who have successfully called their coin flips 20 times in a row and who, by this exercise, each have turned one dollar into a little over $1 million. $225 million would have been lost, $225 million would have been won.*

> *By then, this group will really lose their heads. They will probably write books on 'How I turned a Dollar into a Million in Twenty Days Working Thirty Seconds a Morning.' Worse yet, they'll probably start jetting around the country attending seminars on efficient coin-flipping and tackling skeptical professors with, 'If it can't be done, why are there 215 of us?' By then some business school professor will probably be rude enough to bring up the fact that if 225 million orangutans had engaged in a similar exercise, the results would be much the same – 215 egotistical orangutans with twenty straight winning flips."*[155]

Worse yet is when someone acts recklessly and takes irresponsible risks that somehow manage, against all odds, to turn a profit. The arrogant person attributes his success to his talent and wisdom. The humble person understands that it was just good luck.

> *"Unquestionably, some people have become very rich through the use of borrowed money. However, that's also been a way to get very poor. When leverage works it magnifies your gains. Your spouse thinks you're clever, and your neighbors get envious.*
>
> *Over the years, a number of very smart people have learned the hard way that a long string of impressive numbers multiplied by a single zero always equals zero. Owners naturally would like to believe that their wonderful profitability is achieved only because they unfailingly turn out a wonderful product that comfortable theory wilts before an uncomfortable fact...good or bad a dominant [business] will prosper."*[156]

In 1997 Warren Buffett made $600 million trading zero coupon US treasury bonds. He considered this to be an unconventional investment that he generally would not engage in, but he felt that in this case the odds favored it. In his annual report, he pointed out that it was extremely risky and it could have made him look very foolish. Rather than brag he simply writes,

> *"We will occasionally make an unconventional move when we believe the odds favor it. Try to think kindly of us when we blow one."*

At the end of the forty-year sojourn in the desert, as the Jewish people prepared to enter the land of Israel, Moses gave his farewell address. Moses blessed the people with all forms of material prosperity: nice houses, rich flocks, silver and gold, and they should "eat and be satisfied." Then he issued a solemn warning.

"[When you prosper, be careful that you do not] say to yourselves, 'It was my own strength and personal power that brought me all this prosperity.' You must remember that it is God your Lord who gives you the power to become prosperous. He does this so as to keep the covenant that He made with an oath to your fathers."[157]

Warren Buffett says he is agnostic about God's existence, but he regularly expresses the type of humility that Moses called for.

> *"I've had it so good in this world, you know. The odds were fifty-to-one against me being born in the United States in 1930. I won the lottery the day I emerged from the womb by being in the United States instead of in some other country where my chances would have been way different.*
>
> *Imagine there are two identical twins in the womb, both equally bright and energetic. And the genie says to them, 'One of you is*

going to be born in the United States, and one of you is going to be born in Bangladesh. And if you wind up in Bangladesh, you will pay no taxes. What percentage of your income would you bid to be the one that is born in the United States?' It says something about the fact that society has something to do with your fate and not just your innate qualities. The people who say, 'I did it all myself,' and think of themselves as Horatio Alger – believe me, they'd bid more to be in the United States than in Bangladesh. That's the Ovarian Lottery."[58]

In his book *The Audacity of Hope*, President Barak Obama quotes sage advice about humility from Warren Buffett.

"I happen to have a talent for allocating capital. But my ability to use that talent is completely dependent on the society I was born into. If I'd been born into a tribe of hunters, this talent of mine would be pretty worthless. I can't run very fast. I'm not particularly strong. I'd probably end up as some wild animal's dinner. But I was lucky enough to be born in a time and place where society values my talent, and gave me a good education to develop that talent, and set up the laws and the financial system to let me do what I love doing."

There is still another aspect of humility.

Berkshire Hathaway, currently the name of Warren Buffett's company, was originally the name of a textile mill in New England. Warren Buffett first took control of Berkshire Hathaway in May of 1965 when he was still operating as Buffett Partnership Ltd. In 1985, after successive years of either subpar returns and, by the end, massive losses, Warren Buffett was forced to shut it down.

Berkshire Hathaway was not the worst mistake of his career, but bad investments in the textile industry seemed to be a recurring theme.

> "One more confession and then I'll go on to more pleasant topics: Can you believe that in 1975 I bought Waumbec Mills, another New England textile company? Of course, the purchase price was a 'bargain' based on the assets we received and the projected synergies with Berkshire's existing textile business. Nevertheless – surprise, surprise – Waumbec was a disaster, with the mill having to be closed down not many years later. And now some good news: The northern textile industry is finally extinct. You need no longer panic if you hear that I've been spotted wandering around New England."[159]

Warren Buffett could name his company anything that he wanted to. If he decided to change the name of his company back to "Buffett" tomorrow, I am confident that his shareholders would be okay with that. Why would he choose to name his company after a failed investment?

The Bible is not a list of the accomplishments of the Jewish people. Quite the opposite, the Bible glosses over the accomplishments of the Jewish people and hyper focuses on their errors and misdeeds.

No superlative encomium is showered on the Jewish people when, after almost two centuries of slavery, 600,000 people were able to instantly establish a form of self-governance[160] and assemble into a neatly arranged encampment formation.[161]

By reading the Torah you would think that the Jewish People spent forty years in the desert doing nothing but complaining, when in fact you can count all the times they complained on one hand, and most of those complaints were about serious problems such as not having water to drink.[162]

The Biblical book of Judges together with the book of Kings chronicles about 800 years of Jewish history. The Biblical authors glossed over generations that acted properly with one sentence, "And the land was tranquil for *eighty years*."[163] They devoted the bulk of the content of their books to reminding us of our sins. The Bible is not interested in telling us what we did right. The purpose of the Bible is to tell us what we did wrong, and that we should not make those same mistakes again in the future.

Moses did not record a single word of praise that he personally gave to the Jewish People, only chastisement, reproof, and castigation. Yet to this day Moses remains unrivaled as the greatest and most beloved leader of Jewish history.

I suggest that part of the reason that Warren Buffett continued to call his company Berkshire Hathaway was as a permanent reminder that he is capable of making mistakes. A humble person does not want to constantly hear how great he is. There is not much to be learned from that. Better to go over mistakes and learn from them.

Every year at Berkshire Hathaway's annual shareholders meeting Warren Buffett invites any qualified investor who is currently short selling Berkshire Hathaway stock to address the shareholders and explain his negative projections and what factors he feels will cause the stock to decline.

In the words of King David, "I recognize my iniquity, and my sin is before me always."[164]

In the words of Charlie Munger, "Tell me the bad news, the good news will take care of itself."[165]

Nothing is inevitable, especially when arrogance is present. "Before destruction comes pride, and before stumbling comes a haughty spirit."[166] "But to the Humble He gives favor."[167]

We will issue common stock only when we receive as much in business value as we give. This rule applies to all forms of issuance – not only mergers or public stock offerings, but stock-for-debt swaps, stock options, and convertible securities as well. We will not sell small portions of your company – and that is what the issuance of shares amounts to – on a basis inconsistent with the value of the entire enterprise.

Owner's Manual, Tenth Principle

You shall have just scales, just weights, just dry measures, and just liquid measures.

Leviticus 19:35

Justice, justice shall you pursue.

Deuteronomy 16:20

Treasures of wickedness will not avail, but justice will save from death.

Proverbs 10:2

10

Justice

June 26th 2006,
Mr. and Mrs. William H. Gates III
Bill and Melinda Gates Foundation

Dear Bill and Melinda:

I greatly admire what the Bill & Melinda Gates Foundation ("BMG") is accomplishing and want to materially expand its future capabilities. Accordingly, by this letter, I am irrevocably committing to make annual gifts of Berkshire Hathaway "B" shares throughout my lifetime for the benefit of BMG.

Warren Buffett likes to purchase acquisitions using cash, not by trading Berkshire Hathaway stock for stock in the new business.

> "Trading shares of a wonderful business – which Berkshire most certainly is – for ownership of a so–so business irreparably destroys value... Too often CEOs seem blind to an

elementary reality: The intrinsic value of the shares you give in an acquisition must not be greater than the intrinsic value of the business you receive."[168]

That Warren Buffett committed to give his fortune over to the Bill and Melinda Gates Foundation in the form of stock can only mean that he values their business even more than he values Berkshire Hathaway. And that is saying a lot.

Warren Buffett frequently expresses appreciation for being born into a society that allowed him to prosper, and he feels a debt of gratitude. For that reason he and his wife have always indicated that they would eventually leave a share of their wealth towards the purpose of perpetuating and improving that society so that others in the future will have the opportunity to prosper as he did.

In Judaism this attitude is called '*Tzedakah.*' This Hebrew word is often mistranslated as 'charity.' Giving a portion of your hard earned wealth back to society is not a charitable kindness. It is a debt that you owe. All that you earn comes from God. He entrusts it to you, and expects that you use it wisely, and share a portion of it with those less fortunate.

Warren Buffett's tenth principle states that Berkshire Hathaway only gives away when it receives fair value in return. That is called justice.

Prior to his letter, Warren Buffett had always intended that his wealth would ultimately go towards helping others, but until that point he was not known for his philanthropy. Suddenly in 2006, at a healthy seventy-five years old, he announced to the world that he was giving it all away.

Perhaps he waited so long so that he could not identify a charitable institution that had the capacity to properly absorb his enormous fortune.

"Buffett measured social projects through the same lens as business ventures; he wanted a return."[169]

To give money away indiscriminately can make a philanthropist feel good in the short term, but there is a greater satisfaction when your hard-earned dollars are given to a cause that makes a measurable and lasting impact on people's lives.

Alternatively, it can be devastating when charitable dollars are irresponsibly squandered.

Omaha natives Donald and Mildred Othmer invested $50,000 with Warren Buffett's original partnership in 1961. Just eight years later, their partnership shares were traded in for 14,500 shares of Berkshire Hathaway stock, which at the time was trading at $42 a share. When they died in the mid-nineties, their shares were worth $780 million (if they were alive today their net worth would be over $3 billion).

The Othmers wished for their estate to benefit society, and they willed their massive fortune to be split between a number of institutions, including $135 million to Long Island College Hospital. The Othmers had specified that only income, not principal, was to be spent so that the endowment should last in perpetuity.

Perpetuity came early.

Less than twenty years later the Wall Street Journal reported that the money-losing hospital's owners were given permission to close it down; almost all of the Othmers' money had been spent.

"In a series of court-approved transactions, hospital administrators repeatedly tapped the fund to serve as collateral for loans and to cover malpractice and other costs, according to court records. The transfers were permissible to keep the hospital going, the court ruled, saying that is what the Othmers would have wanted."[170]

The Talmud recounts as one of the most terrible curses, "may your charitable donations be ineffective."[171] When the Othmers bequeathed their fortune to the hospital, they invested more than their money. They invested their trust in the institution, only to be utterly disappointed.

It is a great challenge to find charitable investments that will yield the greatest returns, not in dollars, but in impact.

"In investments you can measure results, with some of this other stuff, you don't know in the end whether you've won or lost."[172]

For this reason, Berkshire Hathaway lets its shareholders vote on where the corporate charitable contributions go. Warren Buffett is opposed to management dictating where shareholders' contributions should be directed.

> *"Neither our operating managers nor officers of the parent company use Berkshire funds to make contributions to broad national programs or charitable activities of special personal interest to them, except to the extent they do so as shareholders. If your employees, including your CEO, wish to give to their alma mater or other institutions to which they feel a personal attachment, we believe they should use their own money, not yours."*[173]

In Jewish tradition, the highest level of charity is to give someone a job, a business loan, or anything that will enable them to become independent of charity. Warren Buffett seems to agree with this philosophy.

In 1971 he pulled his support of a community minority bank when it began to flounder due to irresponsible loans. While others viewed the bank as a method of giving handouts, Warren Buffett wanted the bank to aid successful businesses capable of paying back their debt.

Similarly, Buffett voted for Richard Nixon over George McGovern in the 1972 presidential election. He had initially favored McGovern but changed his mind after McGovern announced his plan to give each person in America a $1,000 a year stipend.[174]

After the death of his wife Susie in 2004, the Buffett foundation was inundated with as much as $40 billion. By law the foundation was obligated to give away a minimum of 5% a year. At that time, the foundation only had a few employees and was not equipped to responsibly give away that kind of money in a way that would make Warren Buffet feel comfortable. He needed to find a charitable foundation that he trusted to partner with.

Fortunately, he found the Bill and Melinda Gates Foundation.

"Bill Gates is the most rational guy around in terms of his foundation. He and Melinda are saving more lives in terms of dollars spent than anybody else. They've worked enormously hard on it. He thinks extremely well. He reads thousands of pages a year on philanthropy and health care. You couldn't have two better people running things. They have done incredible work, they've thought it through, their values are right, their logic is right."[175]

When it comes to his charitable giving, Warren Buffett has critics, most notably, billionaire philanthropist Michael Steinhardt. In an interview given after Warren Buffett's initial gift, Steinhardt said,

"[Buffett's] reality is he is the greatest PR person of recent times and he has managed to achieve a snow job that conned virtually everyone in the press to my knowledge. What he has done...is that he gave away two and a half cents for the first seventy-some-odd years of his life. He gave away nothing and then in one fell swoop he gave away almost all of his money, thoughtlessly, to one guy.

"I gave more away much earlier. It's a good thing that he's giving it away now, but it's not good that [his lack of giving over the years] is not being reflected upon."[176]

Steinhardt's criticism may very well be in line with Jewish principles of *Tzedakah*.

Judaism attributes great value to giving for urgent and pressing causes. If a destitute person approaches you and asks for help, there is an explicit obligation to help him immediately.[177]

The Talmud tells of a great philanthropist named Mar Ukva, and how his wife was considered an even greater philanthropist than he was. When Mar Ukva inquired why, he learned that although his own large communal philanthropic endeavors were praiseworthy, his gifts did not fill the immediate needs of the poor in a timely manner. His wife opened up their home to the poor and gave them money and food directly.[178]

There is also a Jewish value to give every single day. In every Jewish home there is a small box with a slot carved into the top called a pushka. Every Jewish child is trained from the youngest age to insert a coin, even as small as a penny, into the pushka every day.

This custom is not only for the purpose of raising money. The pushka is actually a way to make charitable giving into a habit, an instinct. If you exercise your giving muscles in small doses every day you are more likely to be generous when opportunities present themselves.

Charlie Munger agrees with this approach.

For years he had been regularly giving to different institutions. Although he and Warren Buffett are partners, he was never a contender for the title of richest man on earth like Warren Buffett. On June 13, 2013 Charlie Munger became the only member of the Berkshire Hathaway board of trustees with a net worth of less than $1 Billion (He only had a net worth of $800 million.) He had just given a $2 billion charitable gift. In an interview after his gift, he downplayed his incredible generosity.

"There is nothing less significant than an extra $2 billion to a ninety-year-old man."

In the years before his partnership with the Gates Foundation Warren Buffett was not being stingy. There was a philosophy behind his giving strategy.

> "I always had the idea that philanthropy was important today, but would be equally important in one year, ten years, twenty years, and the future generally. And someone who was compounding money at a high rate, I thought, was the better party to be taking care of philanthropy that was to be done twenty years out, while the people compounding at a lower rate should logically take care of current philanthropy."[79]

The Talmud tells a story about the sage Shmuel whose father managed the finances for a group of orphans. Shmuel learned that

Justice | 117

his father had buried their money in the earth in a sealed tube. The tube had three compartments. Shmuel's father kept their own personal money in the top and bottom compartments, whereas he stored the orphans' money in the middle. When Shmuel asked why, his father answered, "If thieves discover the tube, they will only take from our money. If underground vermin get to the tube, they will only eat away at our money. In both cases the orphans' money is protected."[180]

In a way, since Warren Buffett and his wife had dedicated their fortune to *Tzedakah* early on, it is reasonable to say that they were acting as trustees for money that had already been dedicated for that purpose. One could argue that Warren Buffett's career has really been managing a charitable fund.

Another argument in defense of the Warren Buffett *Tzedakah* philosophy is the attention that it attracted. As Steinhardt himself mentioned, Steinhardt had been giving away hundreds of millions for years and nobody paid attention. But when Warren Buffett gave what amounted to one of the largest single charitable gifts in history, the press noticed. More importantly, other billionaires noticed.

Warren Buffett and Bill Gates used their influence to convince other billionaires to follow their lead by leaving the bulk of their fortunes to charity as well. Warren Buffett and Bill Gates may have done more for charity than anyone in history.

In December 2010, Gates, Buffett and other billionaires signed what they called the "Gates-Buffett Giving Pledge" in which they promised to donate to charity at least half of their wealth over the course of time.

Even Steinhardt had to admit, "[Warren Buffett] became the greatest advocate to philanthropy and pitched all the bumbling billionaires to do the same thing, and many of them did. Now that takes a special guy."[181]

Warren Buffett was interviewed by a secular Israeli when he bought Iscar. The interviewer could not get over Warren Buffett's decision to give away his money to *Tzedakah*. Almost indignantly he asked, "You don't care about money?" The secular Israeli went on to give Warren Buffett a lesson in Jewish values. He said, "In Judaism there is a value to leave [money] over to your children."

Lamentably, this secular Israeli news personality demonstrated his ignorance of Jewish values. While there is certainly a value to make sure that your children are provided for, there is no commandment to leave them billions.

On the contrary, sometimes leaving children too much wealth can have damaging effects. Warren Buffett responded to the Israeli with words of advice that he gives regarding the matter of inheritance, "You should leave your children with enough so that they can do anything, but not too much so that they will do nothing."[182]

Before the death of the great philanthropist Mar Ukva, the Talmud reports that he also gave away most of his estate to charity. When asked why, he said, "The road is long and I need a lot of baggage."[183] He didn't view his *tzedakah*-giving as a liability; he viewed it as an asset that would serve him when he departed from this world.

In a way the secular Israeli reporter was right. Judaism does require that parents leave over something for their children. He was wrong about what that something is. Jews have been around for a long time, and we know as well as any other nation that no matter how you do your estate planning, there are no guarantees when it comes to transferring wealth. Throughout history wealthy Jewish communities found themselves exiled from countries and all of their property confiscated and looted.

There is an inheritance that is far more valuable than money. When the Jewish people speak of inheritance they say, "The Torah that Moses commanded us is the inheritance of the children of Jacob."[184]

You should be fully aware of one attitude Charlie and I share that hurts our financial performance: Regardless of price, we have no interest at all in selling any good businesses that Berkshire owns. We are also very reluctant to sell sub-par businesses as long as we expect them to generate at least some cash and as long as we feel good about their managers and labor relations. We hope not to repeat the capital-allocation mistakes that led us into such sub-par businesses. And we react with great caution to suggestions that our poor businesses can be restored to satisfactory profitability by major capital expenditures. (The projections will be dazzling and the advocates sincere, but, in the end, major additional investment in a terrible industry usually is about as rewarding as struggling in quicksand.) Nevertheless, gin rummy managerial behavior (discard your least promising business at each turn) is not our style. We would rather have our overall results penalized a bit than engage in that kind of behavior.

Owner's Manual, Eleventh Principle

Forgive now the iniquity of this people according to the greatness of Your kindness.

Numbers 14:19

Judge with true justice and perform kindness and mercy towards one another.

Zachariah 7:9

Through kindness and truth iniquity will be forgiven.

Proverbs 16:6

11

Kindness

The name Berkshire Hathaway was originally the name of a textile manufacturer in New England. Warren Buffett first took control of Berkshire in May of 1965 when he was still operating as Buffett Partnership Ltd.

Warren Buffett enjoyed a few years of success with the investment. "Then the honeymoon ended. During the eighteen years following 1966, we struggled unremittingly with the textile business, all to no avail."

During those years the textile industry continued to decline, with every new year bringing increasingly lower annual returns on his investment. Occasionally Buffett thought that investing just a little more capital might turn the failing business around. But as he himself has said many times, "turnarounds seldom turn."[185]

Each investment would just barely keep Berkshire up to speed with its many competitors.

> *"It was like each person watching a parade deciding simultaneously that if they stand on their tiptoes they will be able to see a little better."*[186]

During the last five years of operation, the textile industry was in freefall. Two hundred and fifty other mills had closed and Berkshire Hathaway's losses were $5 million.

Over that time Warren Buffett only approved capital expenditures on the textile operation if they were absolutely necessary. Any other cash generated by the mill was diversified into other investments such as banks, newspapers, and insurance companies.

The shareholders questioned Warren Buffett's wisdom in keeping the plant open so long.

Throughout those years Warren Buffett reiterated his reasons for staying in the business.

> *(1) our textile businesses are very important employers in their communities. Our mills in both New Bedford and Manchester are among the largest employers in each town, utilizing a labor force of high average age possessing relatively non–transferable skills. (2) management has been straightforward in reporting on problems and energetic in attacking them, (3) labor has been cooperative and understanding in facing our common problems, and (4) the business should average modest cash returns relative to investment.*"[187]

He further said,

> "*As long as these conditions prevail – and we expect that they will – we intend to continue to support our textile business despite more attractive alternative uses for capital.*"

It turned out that he was wrong about (4), and in 1985 Warren Buffett finally shut down Berkshire Hathaway. According to Ken

Chase, the loyal manager Warren Buffett tapped to run the plant, Warren Buffett kept Berkshire Hathaway opened ten years longer than he should have.[188]

By regular investment standards, Warren Buffett would have been completely justified to shut down Berkshire years earlier. Doing so would have been acceptable according to the standard of strict justice.

In the case of Berkshire Hathaway Warren Buffett held himself to a higher standard than strict justice. In Hebrew we would say that he went beyond *tzedek* - justice. He showed the attribute of *chesed* - kindness.

The eleventh principle states that strict justice is not always the standard to be followed. There are circumstances that call for extending yourself beyond the minimum requirement and giving more. That is called kindness.

The Torah commands us to "do what is right and good,"[189] and to "be holy."[190] Regarding these verses, the medieval Jewish philosopher Nachmanides wrote, "It is conceivable to be a wicked person while still acting in conformity with the laws of the Torah. For that reason the Torah includes general injunctions like 'do what is right and good' and 'be holy' to instruct us that in all matters, one should do what is 'good and right', including even compromise and going beyond the letter of the law."[191]

One Talmudic opinion goes as far as to say that a person who acts with the attitude of "what is mine is mine and what is yours is yours," is acting in accordance with the culture of the wicked Biblical cities of Sodom and Gomorrah.[192]

The Talmudic sage Rabbi Yochanan said that Jerusalem fell to the Romans because the Jewish people were conducting themselves only according to strict justice, without kindness.[193]

Kindness does not mean pure altruism, living completely for others. King Solomon tells us, "One who does good for himself is a man of kindness."[194] The Talmud forbids a person from giving money to charity if it will then cause him to be dependent upon others. Giving away more than twenty percent to charity is considered to be extravagant.[195] There is a moral imperative to take care of your own needs before caring for the needs of others.[196]

As the great sage Hillel said, "If I am not for myself, then who will be for me?"[197]

> *"I won't close down a business of subnormal profitability merely to add a fraction of a point to our corporate rate of return. However, I also feel it inappropriate for even an exceptionally profitable company to fund an operation once it appears to have unending losses in prospect. Adam Smith would disagree with my first proposition and Karl Marx would disagree with my second; the middle ground is the only position that leaves me comfortable...*
>
> *I ignored Comte's advice, 'The intellect should be the servant to the heart – but not its slave.'"*[198]

The great Zionist thinker Zev Jabotinsky touched on this concept in his writings about social philosophy in what would soon be the modern state of Israel. The Torah mandates that once in every fifty year period there shall be proclaimed a freedom year; any family that has been forced by poverty to sell their land shall recover it, and any person who was forced by poverty to sell himself into slavery shall be freed.

In the 19th century, A.S. Lieberman, one of the fathers of Jewish socialism, wrote, "For us, socialism is not strange. The commune is the basis of the Torah which has made concrete in the laws that land is not to be sold in perpetuity, in the law of the Jubilee year."[199]

Jabotinsky vociferously objected. The jubilee concept acknowledges and allows for the "free play of economic forces and the competitive order of the world's economy which causes one man to win and another to lose." The laws of the Torah lean towards Adam Smith, but periodically, in the case of the Jubilee once in a generation, the Torah will violate strict capitalist principles and interfere by injecting kindness into the market to protect members of society from entering into an intergenerational cycle of poverty that becomes increasingly harder to break.[200]

Corporate raiders who buy and sell companies on a dime often leave a trail of destruction in their wake. Sometimes thousands of jobs are lost and lives are ruined as the liquidators enrich themselves at the expense of others.

Warren Buffett is a builder. He strengthens the companies he invests in, and he profits as his companies create jobs, while providing quality goods and services to their customers. He contributes to the building of the world, and as the Psalmist said, "The world will be built on kindness."[201]

We will be candid in our reporting to you, emphasizing the pluses and minuses important in appraising business value. Our guideline is to tell you the business facts that we would want to know if our positions were reversed. We owe you no less.

Moreover, as a company with a major communications business, it would be inexcusable for us to apply lesser standards of accuracy, balance and incisiveness when reporting on ourselves than we would expect our news people to apply when reporting on others. We also believe candor benefits us as managers: The CEO who misleads others in public may eventually mislead himself in private.

Owner's Manual, Twelfth Principle

Stay far away from falsehood.

Exodus 23:7

Anyone who is dishonest is an abomination to God your Lord.

Deuteronomy 25:16

The crown of your words is truth.

Psalms 119:160

12

Honesty

Ten years after Warren Buffett purchased the Nebraska Furniture Mart, he found another Rose Blumkin. His name was Harold Alfond. Born in Swampscott, MA in 1914 to Russian Jewish immigrants, at the age of twenty Alfond began his career working at a local shoe factory for twenty-five cents an hour. In 1956 he opened his own factory in Dexter, ME with $10,000 of capital. By 1993 Dexter Shoes was producing seven and a half million pairs of shoes a year. Warren Buffett purchased the company for $443 million - and he thought he found a bargain.

> *"[Charlie and I] promptly jumped at the chance last year to acquire Dexter Shoe of Dexter, Maine, which manufactures popular-priced men's and women's shoes. Dexter, I can assure you, needs no fixing: It is one of the best-managed companies Charlie and I have seen in our business lifetimes."*[202]

Despite Warren Buffett's optimism about the acquisition, he went on to mention that there were three catches to the deal.

The first catch was shoes were an industry that was outside of Warren Buffett's circle of competence. He justified this uncharacteristic move based on a previous acquisition that was proving successful. Berkshire had purchased its first shoe manufacturer, H. and H. Brown, in 1991, and was making good money from the investment.

> *"Five years ago we had no thought of getting into shoes. Now we have 7,200 employees in that industry...In 1994, we expect Berkshire's shoe operations to have more than $550 million in sales...and I sing "There's No Business Like Shoe Business" as I drive to work."*[203]

Dexter Shoes was an add-on to an earlier investment that already seemed to be working.

The second catch was the threat of foreign shoe manufacturers, but Warren Buffett had confidence in his shoe companies.

> *"The domestic shoe industry is generally thought to be unable to compete with imports from low–wage countries. But someone forgot to tell this to the ingenious managements of Dexter and H. H. Brown and to their skilled labor forces, which together make the U.S. plants of both companies highly competitive against all comers."*

Warren Buffett wagered that his domestic shoe companies could keep up with foreign imports, and that the demand for foreign made shoes would wane over time. He was wrong on both counts.

> *"I was wrong about the economic future of that one. The people working in the town of Dexter, Maine were wonderful*

people who were very good at what they did. But even if they were twice as good as the Chinese, the Chinese would work for a tenth as much."[204]

After only eight years, Warren Buffett folded what was left of Dexter Shoes into his other shoe investments, shut down their U.S. operations, and moved them overseas.

In 2007 Warren Buffett wrote that Dexter was the worst acquisition he had ever made.

But the third and biggest catch was in the terms of the deal itself.

Normally Warren Buffett makes purchases in cash, but the Alfond family was not interested in cash. Instead, they and the other shareholders of Dexter exchanged their shares in Dexter for 25,203 shares of Berkshire Hathaway class A stock.

"By using Berkshire stock, I compounded this error hugely. That move made the cost to Berkshire shareholders not $400 million, but rather $3.5 billion. In essence, I gave away 1.6% of a wonderful business – one now valued at $220 billion – to buy a worthless business."[205]

To admit a mistake that is obvious to all is easy, and it is not hard to confess to a misdeed after being caught in the act. But there are some mistakes that are not immediately apparent to others that can be glossed over or swept under the rug. To admit to those mistakes is challenging. It requires true honesty.

Warren Buffett is the first one to call out hidden mistakes. Most notably, he regularly calls attention to his investment of $4 million for 5% of Disney in 1966 which he sold a few years later for

$6 million. That error, which does not show up on his balance sheets, cost Berkshire Hathaway billions of dollars.

Generally Accepted Accounting Principles do not reflect these errors, and the average shareholder probably would not notice them either. Warren Buffett takes his responsibility to his shareholders seriously. He is honest with them, and he holds himself accountable for both mistakes of commission, and mistakes of omission.

> *"For me and my partner Charlie Munger, the biggest mistakes have not been mistakes of commission, they have been mistakes of omission. We knew enough about the business to do something, and for one reason or another we sat there sucking our thumbs instead of doing something. We have passed up things where we could have made billions of dollars for things that we understood. The fact that we could have made billions from Microsoft doesn't mean anything because I could never understand Microsoft. But I understood healthcare stocks, I should have made money but I didn't. I should have made money on Fannie Mae in the 80s and I didn't. Those are billion dollar mistakes that Generally Accepted accounting principles don't pick up."*[206]

The twelfth principle requires that when evaluating your conduct you do so with complete honesty and provide the whole truth to those whom you are accountable to, and to yourself.

The attribute of honesty also demands that you do your best to live up to your contractual expectations. If you fall short of those expectations, whether or not it was your fault, you are required to report honestly to those who were counting on you.

In Jewish tradition theft is more than the act of reaching into the pocket of your neighbor and stealing his wallet. An hourly employee who is idle when he should be working is considered to be a thief.

When the Biblical Jacob was confronted by his employer, his father-in-law Laban, Jacob said, "These twenty years I have spent in your service, your ewes and goats never miscarried, nor did I feast on rams from your flock. That which was torn by beast I never brought to you; I myself made good on the loss...I was ravaged by scorching heat by day and frost by night; and sleep fled from my eyes."[207]

This declaration was meant to serve as an example forever for the descendants of Jacob of how you must work for an employer. You are required to do your absolute best, live up to the terms of your agreement, and provide full value for the time you are employed. That is honesty.

Rabbi Moses Chaim Luzzatto speaks about this at length in his work *The Path of the Just*.

"The rule in this matter is that anyone who contracts with a friend for any type of work, every hour that he is hired to him belong to his friend....and anything that he takes from those hours for his own benefit is nothing but pure theft."[208]

Even if you perform a good deed instead of working, if the deed was performed on your employer's time it is not considered to be a good deed. It is a sin.

Warren Buffett constantly decries dishonesty in reporting.

> *"There are managers who actively use Generally Accepted Accounting Principles (GAAP) to deceive and defraud. They*

> *know that many investors and creditors accept GAAP results as gospel. So these charlatans interpret the rules 'imaginatively' and record business transactions in ways that technically comply with GAAP but actually display an economic illusion to the world."*[209]

The Torah says that Jacob's brother Esau "knew how to trap," and would "trap his father Isaac by using his mouth."[210] The commentator Rashi cites a Jewish tradition that explains how Esau would deceive his father. He would ask his father nuanced questions of morality such as, "Father, when I am tithing for charity, must I also separate from items such as salt and straw?" By inquiring about the extremities of the law, Esau gave his father the impression that he was meticulous with charity. Based on his conversations with Esau, Isaac assumed that Esau was constantly involved in charity, meanwhile Esau was going out and murdering people. He didn't bother to ask his father if that was kosher.

In his letter to shareholders in 1990 Warren Buffett published a satire written by Benjamin Graham in 1935. It is a fictional letter from a fictional company announcing a "sweeping modernization scheme." The company was operating at a loss of $3 per share. The chairman announces that the company will not be changing any of its manufacturing or selling policies. Instead, the bookkeeping system will be entirely revamped. By using a variety of Generally Accepted Accounting Principles in an extreme way he creates a balance sheet based on the same previous year, but instead of reporting a loss of $3 a share, the company reports a profit of $50 a share.

> *"Specifically, sellers and their representatives invariably present financial projections having more entertainment value than educational value."*[211]

To illustrate this idea, Warren Buffett has a parable about a man with an ailing horse.

> *"Visiting the vet, he said, 'Can you help me? Sometimes my horse walks just fine and sometimes he limps.' The vet's reply was pointed: 'No problem — when he's walking fine, sell him.'"*[212]

Of all attributes, Warren Buffett is probably most known for his honesty, both in the way that he reports to his shareholders, and in his vigilance to stay away from deals that have even the slightest traces of dishonesty.

Probably the most dramatic episode in his career was the Salomon Brothers Scandal of 1991. It was discovered that Salomon's bond trading division had been engaged in highly unethical activities, and it was clear that some of Salomon's top managers were aware of the activity and had covered it up. At the time Warren Buffett was a major shareholder and a member of the board, but Warren Buffett was not responsible for, and could not be held accountable for, the surreptitious misdeeds of the bond trader. On top of that, the nature of his investment in Salomon insulated him from the financial consequences of a bankruptcy.

"The safe thing [for Buffett] would be to give Salomon a quiet burial. True, Buffett had a $700 million investment in Salomon preferred. But the preferred stock was far safer than the common;

neither Munger nor Buffett thought they would lose much money in a liquidation."[213]

Nevertheless Warren Buffett made a fateful decision to step into the breech and take the reins of Salomon as interim chairman.

If Salomon went down, Warren Buffett's financial losses would be limited, but the damage to his reputation would be irreparable. The money was fungible and could always be made again. But as he frequently says, "It takes a lifetime to build a reputation and five minutes to ruin it."[214]

Warren Buffett took the stand as a witness in a congressional hearing. He began with an apology.

"I would like to start by apologizing for the acts that have brought us here. The Nation has a right to expect its rules and laws are obeyed. At Salomon, certain of these were broken."[215]

The Bible contrasts the behavior of two kings, King Saul and King David, when each was respectively caught in a scandal.

King Saul was commanded by the prophet Samuel to wage war against and completely wipe out the nation of Amalek. This evil nation had been involved in acts of terrorism and attempted genocide since the Jewish people left Egypt, and had continued to harass the Jews any time they had the chance for the next 400 years. Samuel specifically commanded King Saul even to kill their livestock, presumably so that there should be no suspicion that the motive was for profit rather than security and justice.

King Saul, in a moment of weakness, spared the animals and allowed his soldiers to plunder them. When the prophet Samuel came to greet him after the victory Saul said, "I have fulfilled the Lord's command." To which the prophet answered sarcastically, "Then what is the bleating of the sheep in my ears?"

Realizing that he was caught, King Saul began to give excuses, "The troops spared the choicest of the sheep for the Lord!" But Samuel would hear no excuses. He chastised the King and proclaimed that his Kingdom would be removed and given over to another.[216]

Years later, King David had an affair with Bat Sheba, a married woman. The affair was neatly covered up, and Bat Sheba's husband Uriah, a soldier, was sent to the front lines and killed in battle. King David then married Bat Sheba. It was the perfect crime. No questions were asked, no suspicions were raised, and King David had plausible deniability.

The incident became known to the prophet Nathan. He confronted King David about his crime. King David could have denied the incident, or offered any number of excuses for his actions. All he said was, "I have sinned before the Lord." He was punished for his crime, but because of his honesty he maintained his kingdom.[217]

As interim chairman Warren Buffett took radical steps to earn back Salomon's reputation, including turning over the most damning evidence of wrongdoing to the Securities and Exchange Commission, against the advice of Salomon's lawyers. All of those in top management who were involved in the cover up were fired.

Next he fired Salomon's paid political consultants and ended all political donations. He did not want to give the appearance that Salomon was buying favors from Washington.

"Salomon brothers would have to do more than obey the rules. Anything not only on the line, but near the line, will be called out."[218]

Charlie Munger says, "We think there should be a huge area between what you are willing to do and what you can do without significant risk of suffering criminal penalty or causing losses. We believe you shouldn't go anywhere near that line. There should be all kinds of things you won't do even though they are perfectly legal. That's the way that we try to operate."[219]

The Talmud teaches that the person who would sweep the Temple treasury room was forbidden from entering if he was wearing shoes or wearing pants with pockets or cuffs.[220] This was so that nobody should suspect him of stealing, or as the Torah says, "To be clean in the eyes of God and man."[221]

Warren Buffett expects all of his employees to conduct themselves with complete honesty.

"I want employees to ask themselves whether they are willing to have any contemplated act appear on the front page of their local paper the next day, to be read by their spouses, children, and friends.. Lose money and I will be understanding, lose a shred of reputation and I will be ruthless."[222]

The Talmud records that when the great sage Rabbi Yochanan Ben Zakkai was on his death bed, his students asked him to bless them. He blessed them that they should fear God as much as they fear men. The students were puzzled. Is that all? Shouldn't we fear God more than we fear men? He answered them, "See how people will refrain from sin when others are looking."[223]

The Talmud teaches that we should always conduct ourselves as if we are being watched and our acts are being recorded, and sites the Biblical story of Ruth to emphasize this point. A series of unfortunate events had cast Ruth from a prestigious and prosperous household to the status of a beggar, until she found herself in the field of her late husband's cousin Boaz. Boaz, a wealthy landowner, graciously took her in, however, the Bible records that he offered her only a morsel of bread to dip in vinegar. Says the Talmud, had Boaz realized that his actions were being recorded and would be included in scripture and read over by millions of people over thousands of years, instead of giving her meager accommodations he would have prepared a lavish feast in her honor.[224]

The Talmudic sage Akavya ben Mahalalel taught, "Contemplate three things and you will never come into the hands of sin: know what is above you, an eye that sees, an ear that hears, and all your deeds are being recorded in a book."[225]

When it comes to honesty, Warren Buffett and Charlie Munger believe that in the long run honesty is profitable.

"Of course, it is hard to know your own motivations. But I'd like to believe that we'd all behave well even if it didn't work so well financially. And every once in a while we get an opportunity to behave that way. But more often we've made extra money out of morality. Ben Franklin didn't say honesty is the best morals, he said it was the best policy."[226]

Charlie Munger may as well have been quoting directly from Jewish tradition. When advising his son to follow the ways of the Torah, King Solomon assured him that doing the right thing comes with certain benefits. "Length of days is in its right hand; in its left are riches and honor."[227] The Talmudic commentary to this verse explains that those who engage in the ways of the Torah for their own sake will have length of days and surely riches and honor, but those who engage in it for ulterior motives will not merit length of days, but will nevertheless acquire riches and honor.

Warren Buffett is known for his honesty, and in his speeches, writings, and actions he has sought to promote a culture of honesty for its own sake, but also because a culture of honesty is profitable for everyone. Conversely, a culture that rewards dishonesty leads to destruction.

You don't need to look any further than the financial crisis of 2008. Bundles of worthless mortgages were packaged and sold over and over. It was no different from the allegory of the old Hong Kong Sardine Dodge.

During a famine in China, a Hong Kong merchant sold a sardine can filled with mud to another merchant, who sold it at a profit to a third merchant, who sold it at a profit to a fourth, who then sold it on to a fifth. The hapless fifth merchant opened the can and found it to be filled with mud. He returned to the man who sold it to him and demanded his money back. The seller refused and retorted, "Why did you have to open the can?"

"He who robs his father and mother and says, 'this is not a sin,' is the accomplice to the destroyer."[228]

The Bible says that the flood in the days of Noah came to destroy the world because of the sin of theft. Jewish tradition explains that it was a particular kind of theft. People would not steal outright. Rather, if a man was carrying a basket of grapes through the marketplace, each person who passed him would furtively reach out and steal a single grape. By the time the man reached his destination his basket would be completely empty.[229]

The allegory is meant to teach that in a world with a culture of dishonesty, a world where people have no inhibitions about cheating another person so long as they don't get caught, it becomes impossible to do business. A culture of corruption leads to instability and as a result everyone suffers.

Honesty is more than morality. It is the foundation of the world.

Warren Buffett jokes that there is a certain type of depreciation that Berkshire Hathaway suffers from that is not reflected by GAAP.

> *"Finally, there is the negative that recurs annually: Charlie Munger, Berkshire's Vice Chairman and my partner, and I are a year older than when we last reported to you. Mitigating this adverse development is the indisputable fact that the age of your top managers is increasing at a considerably lower rate percentage–wise than is the case at almost all other major corporations. Better yet, this differential will widen in the future."*[230]

Warren Buffett's reputation has only improved with age, like a fine wine. As he and Charlie Munger get older they continue to provide the rest of the world with examples of how honesty pays.

They both assure their shareholders that Berkshire will continue to be strong after they are gone. What they built was built on honesty, and honesty endures forever.

Despite our policy of candor, we will discuss our activities in marketable securities only to the extent legally required. Good investment ideas are rare, valuable and subject to competitive appropriation just as good product or business acquisition ideas are. Therefore we normally will not talk about our investment ideas. This ban extends even to securities we have sold (because we may purchase them again) and to stocks we are incorrectly rumored to be buying. If we deny those reports but say "no comment" on other occasions, the no–comments become confirmation.

Owner's Manual, Thirteenth Principle

There is a time to speak and a time to remain silent

Ecclesiastes 3:7

Silence is a fence for wisdom.

Rabbi Akiva[231]

If a word is worth one coin then silence is worth two.

Rabbi Dimi[232]

13

Silence

The Sun Valley Conference, hosted by the investment firm Allen and Co., is the single largest gathering of the world's megawealthy. At the conference in 1999 there was over a trillion dollars of capital represented there. In 1999 a trillion dollars could purchase all of the real estate in New York, Chicago, and Los Angeles combined. Every year since its inception in 1983 the conference brings together some of the biggest names in business, politics, media, and philanthropy.

Nineteen ninety nine was no different, except there was a new cadre of attendees that year: mostly young, all of them newly wealthy, and completely unknown a year before. These young multi-millionaires made their recent fortunes precipitously as pioneers in the new world heralded in by the internet.

The conference organizer, Herbert Allen, asked Warren Buffett to deliver the keynote address. These young internet tycoons looked on with a bit of skepticism, if not contempt.

True, Warren Buffett had a good run in the past, but he had not jumped on the internet bandwagon. His portfolio did not contain a single company that ended with dotcom. He had missed the boat by not investing in their sexy new companies with non-existent earnings that were soaring to unprecedented heights. Meanwhile, the market prices of the types of companies that comprised Warren Buffett's portfolio, along with the price of Berkshire Hathaway stock, were steadily declining. These technology gurus viewed Warren Buffett as an old dinosaur who stubbornly stuck to his old outdated ways. He just didn't know how to adapt to the ever changing brave new world.

Warren Buffett's lecture that year at the Sun Valley conference served as a response to these claims, a prescient vision of things to come, and a timeless lesson.

> *"The car was probably the most important invention of the first half of the twentieth century. It had an enormous impact on people's lives. If you had seen at the time of the first cars how this country would develop in connection with autos, you would have said, 'This is the place I must be.' But of the two thousand companies, as of a few years ago, only three car companies survived. And at one time or another, all three were selling for less than book value. So autos had an enormous impact on America, but in the opposite direction on investors.*
>
> *Now the other great invention of the first half of the twentieth century was the airplane. In the period from 1919 to 1939, there were about two hundred companies. Imagine if you could have seen the future of the airline industry back there in Kitty Hawk, you would have seen a world undreamed of. But assume you had the insight and you saw all of these people wishing to fly and visit their relatives or run away from their relatives or whatever you do in an airplane, and you decided this was the place to be. As of a couple of years ago, there had been zero*

money made from the aggregate of all stock investment in the airline industry in history. So I submit to you, I really like to think that if I had been down in Kitty Hawk, I would have been farsighted enough and public spirited enough to have shot Orville down. I owed it to future capitalists."[233]

During the market run up in the late 90s it was hard not to get caught up in the frenzy. Watching the stocks of exciting new internet companies rise every day, and seeing people become paper millionaires overnight made it tempting for anyone to jump into the market. Many people who knew nothing about investing did just that. And they were burned.

Warren Buffett's lecture gives us perspective. Sometimes it pays to be patient.

The example of airline companies was something that Warren Buffett could speak to from his own personal experience.

According to Jewish tradition, God challenges each person with an evil inclination that beckons us to sin. Every person's evil inclination is different. Some people are drawn to drink, others to gambling, and others to promiscuity.

Warren Buffett would say that his evil inclination is investing in airlines.

"I made a mistake buying U.S. Air preferred. I had a lot of money around. I make mistakes when I get cash. I hang around the office and I have money in my pocket and I make mistakes. It happens every time. I now have an 800 number that I call every time I think about buying an airline. They talk me down. I say, 'Hi I'm Warren and I'm an air-a-holic.' and the guy on the other end says, 'keep talking, stay on the phone, don't do anything rash!' until finally I get over it."[234]

The students in the academy of the Talmudic sage Rabbi Ishmael used to say, "When the evil inclination beckons you to sin you should run to the study hall."[235]

Warren Buffett says when the evil inclination beckons him to make an investment out of boredom, Charlie Munger tells him to go to a bar instead.[236]

"If they beckon to you, 'Come and join us we will ambush, all kinds of treasure are waiting.' My son, don't go with them. Hold back your feet from their path."[237]

Being good is only part of the equation. The Psalmist tells us first stay away from bad, and then do good.[238]

About his regrettable investment in Salomon brothers Warren Buffett said in retrospect,

> *"It was a nine percent security in a business that I would never have bought the common stock. I should have sat around and bought more Coke."*[239]

What's needed in these situations is the discipline to sit on your hands and not act.

In his modern classic novel *Shogun*, author James Clavell called that the virtue of patience.

"Patience means holding back your inclination to the seven emotions: hate, adoration, joy, anxiety, anger, grief, fear. If you don't give way to the seven, you're patient, then you'll soon understand all manner of things and be in harmony with Eternity."[240]

Jewish ethical literature understands patience in the realm of deed, and more often in the realm of speech. The thirteenth principle states that there are times to speak out and to act, and there are times when the best thing to do is absolutely nothing. Knowing the difference is the virtue of silence.

The Talmudic sage Rabbi Shimon said that he grew up with the wise and he learned that there is nothing better than silence.[241] The commentaries explain that there is a temptation to speak when you are in the company of wise men, to contribute to the conversation and to demonstrate your own intelligence. But there is so much more to be gained by showing restraint, listening instead of talking, and learning from others.

There are times when we have no choice but to speak up. When the righteous, innocent, and helpless are being slandered we must speak out in their defense. To stay idle would be a sin and a violation of the commandment, "do not stand on your brother's blood."[242] In situations like those, silence is forbidden.

There are other times when a decision to speak out of haste can cause more damage than good. Silence may be the most difficult of all virtues because it is so hard to know when it should be applied. Often, however, when in doubt it pays to err on the side of silence.

Warren Buffett admits that some of his biggest mistakes were mistakes of omission, times when he should have acted and spoken up, but instead he remained silent.

He admits that he missed Fannie Mae. He missed health care. These were areas inside his circle of competence, and he should have acted at the right time and made money. These were missed opportunities.

"But there is an advantage in life over Ted Williams. Unlike Ted Williams, we will never be called out for just standing at the plate and not swinging. So why not just stand there?"[243]

Warren Buffett says that you should view your life as a punch card. You only have so many investments so make it count.[244]

Sometimes you will let a fat pitch go by and you just stood there without swinging. When that happens, the most important thing to do is to shake it off. Have no regrets, learn from your mistake, and have faith. There will be other opportunities in the future, just be ready for them.

Warren Buffett is markedly different from the instant dotcom billionaires at the Sun Valley conference. His fortune did not come overnight. He made 99% of his wealth after his fiftieth birthday, and 95% of his wealth after his sixtieth. He was diligent, constant, and patient. He picked his spots carefully. He may have missed some opportunities along the way, but he knew that new opportunities would present themselves down the road. "We never look back because there are so many things to look forward to."[245]

His track record shows that his discipline, his patience, and his silence paid off in the end.

Investing in Values

Warren Buffett spends a great deal of time every year addressing groups of students. This is just one more example of how Warren Buffett invests, in this case by sharing his wisdom with the next generation of business leaders in the hopes that they will continue his legacy of making the world a better place.

He often begins his talks with a mental exercise.

"Play a game with me. I would like for the moment to have you pretend I made you a great offer. You could pick anyone of your classmates and you get 10% of their earnings for the rest of their lives."

He then asks them to play the same game in the reverse and to think about who they would pick if they could sell short someone in their class.

When making those decisions, an intelligent investor would not look for physical characteristics like height or looks, and would not even look at easily measurable metrics like the best grades or the biggest bank account.

"I think that in the end you would pick some individual who has a bunch of qualities that are self-made...qualities like honesty, integrity, and generosity."[246]

The intelligent investor would invest in values.

He then takes the exercise a step further.

"Look at that list and say, is there anything on that list that I couldn't do. And there won't be."

As cliché as it sounds, there are more important things in life than money. "Not by bread alone does man live, rather by every word that comes from the mouth of God."[247] Money alone will not lead to a life of happiness, nor is wealth a sufficient indicator as to whether someone is worthy of admiration. The principles of Warren Buffett represent character traits that are attainable to everyone, but there are no short cuts. These traits can only be acquired through time and effort devoted to character development. If you pursue them, you will find that the time and effort expended will be an investment that will pay valuable dividends indefinitely.

"There is treasure and wealth in the house, but righteousness endures forever."[248]

I wrote this book with a specific purpose in mind. This book is for my children.

I want them to know that a person is measured not by their net worth but by their values. Warren Buffett as a billionaire is only memorable until someone else becomes a trillionaire. If he is to be remembered in the future it will not be for his wealth, but for his wisdom and for his values.

While researching this book I was constantly inspired to work on my own character, and I am grateful to Warren Buffett for that.

My hope is that this book inspires others as well.

I want to express my appreciation to Warren Buffett for all of the wisdom that he has already given and continues to give to the world. Fortunate is our generation to have a cultural icon like Warren Buffett who teaches us these important lessons.

God bless Warren Buffett. May he continue to enjoy health and success so that he can continue with his generosity and good deeds, and so that we can continue to learn from his wisdom.

> *"Lest we end on a bad note, if enjoying life promotes longevity, Methuselah's record is in jeopardy."*[249]

Watch out Methuselah! May Warren Buffett smash his record!

References

Is Warren Buffett Jewish?

1. Samuel Rosenblatt, *Yossele Rosenblatt: A Biography* (Farrar, 1954), 160
2. Proverbs 10:5
3. Proverbs 11:15
4. Proverbs 11:24
5. Proverbs 8:11
6. Annual Letter 2008
7. Numbers 13
8. Irving M. Bunim, *Ethics from Sinai: An Eclectic Wide-ranging Commentary on Pirke Avoth*, (Feldheim, 1966), Vol.2, 152
9. Pirkei Avot 4:21

The Thirteen Principles of Warren Buffett

10. Babylonian Talmud, Makot 24a
11. Comment to Genesis 1:1
12. Psalms 15
13. Proverbs 6:16
14. Pirkei Avot 5:9
15. Babylonian Talmud, Avodah Zarah 20b
16. Benjamin Franklin, *The Autobiography of Benjamin Franklin*, (Gryphon, 1995), 102

FAITH

17	Habakkuk 2:4
18	Babylonian Talmud, Makot 24a
19	Annual Letter 1987
20	Annual Letter 2013
21	Warren Buffett, *The Superinvestors of Graham and Doddsville*
22	Owner's Manual
23	Owner's Manual
24	Benjamin Graham, *The Intelligent Investor: The Definitive Book on Value Investing, A Book of Practical Counsel* (Revised Edition), (Collins, 2006)
25	Annual Letter 2013
26	Annual Letter 1988
27	Warren Buffett, Lecture, University of Florida, October 15, 1998
28	Owner's Manual
29	Exodus 4:1
30	Judah Halevi, *The Kuzari: An Argument for the Faith of Israel* (Schocken, 1964), 44
31	Exodus 20:2
32	Exodus 34:9
33	Annual Letter 2013
34	Annual Letter 2000
35	Exodus 32:4
36	Rashion Exodus 32:6
37	Annual Letter 1992
38	Isaiah 1:11
39	Nechama Leibowitz, *Studies in Exodus* (World Zionist Organization, 1981), 613
40	Annual Letter 2011
41	Pirkei Avot 4:27
42	Pirkei Avot 2:6
43	Roger Lowenstein, *Buffett: The Making of an American Capitalist*, (Random House, 1974), 11
44	Babylonian Talmud, Brachot 63a
45	Annual Letter 2004

46	Youtube.com "Warren Buffett Explains Purchase of Burlington Northern Santa Fe Railroad (April 1, 2011)"
47	Deuteronomy 30:20
48	Babylonian Talmud, Brachot 61b

INTEGRITY

49	Pirkei Avot 2:17
50	Babylonian Talmud, Brachot 28a
51	Robert P. Miles, *The Warren Buffett CEO: Secrets from the Berkshire Hathaway Managers*, (John Wileyand Sons, 2002), 9
52	Annual Letter 1990
53	Annual Letter 1998
54	Leviticus 24:22
55	Deuteronomy 17:14
56	Maimonides Laws of Kings 3:1
57	Babylonian Talmud, Brachot 28a
58	Owner's Manual
59	Owner's Manual
60	Pirkei Avot 1:3
61	Genesis 3:17–19
62	Midrash Rabbah, 20:10
63	Babylonian Talmud, Brachot 28b

QUALITY

64	Babylonian Talmud, Brachot 33b
65	Youtube.com "Interview with Warren Buffett on Buying Iskar with Yaakov Eilon"
66	Annual Letter 2006
67	Natan Sharansky, *Defending Identity: Its Indispensable Role in Defending Democracy* (Public Affairs, 2008), 143
68	Exodus 30:12
69	Annual Letter 1988
70	Exodus 18:22
71	Babylonian Talmud, Yevamot 49b
72	Pirkei Avot 2:1

73	Proverbs 15:23
74	Proverbs 3:2

Simplicity

75	Babylonian Talmud, Kedushin 82b
76	Alice Schroeder, *The Snowball: Warren Buffett and the Business of Life* (Bantam, 2008), 501
77	Annual Letter 1980
78	Schroeder, *Snowball*, 495
79	Cf. Annual Letter 1994
80	Cf. Three Lectures by Warren Buffett at Notre Dame, 1991. Edited by Whitney Tilson http://www.tilsonfunds.com/BuffettNotreDame.pdf
81	Roger Lowenstein, *When Genius Failed: The Rise and Fall of Long Term Capital Management* (Random House, 2001), 233
82	*Poor Charlie's Almanac: The Wit and Wisdom of Charles T. Munger* (abridged edition), Edited by Peter D. Kaufman, (Davis Advisors, 2005), 157
83	Exodus 13:8
84	Proverbs 22:6
85	Exodus 13:14
86	Pirkei Avot 2:6
87	Genesis 6:9
88	Genesis 17:1
89	Genesis 25:27
90	Job 1:1
91	Genesis 25:27
92	Annual Letter 1990
93	Babylonian Talmud, Bava Metzia 75b
94	Deuteronomy 18:13

Insight

95	Pirkei Avot 4:27
96	Warren Buffett, Lecture, Notre Dame, 1991
97	Annual Letter 1985
98	Pirkei Avot 4:20

99	Annual Letter 2013
100	Annual Letter 1979
101	Lowenstein, *Buffett*, 330
102	1 Samuel 16:7
103	Babylonian Talmud, Sotah 14a
104	Owner's Manual
105	Lowenstein, *Buffett*, 281
106	Annual Letter 1989
107	Pirkei Avot 3:12
108	Babylonian Talmud, Megillah 28b
109	Bunim, *Ethics from Sinai*, vol.1, 281
110	Youtube.com, "Interview with Warren Buffett on Buying Iskar with Yaakov Eilon"
111	Rabbi Jonathan Sachs, *To Heal a Fractured World: The Ethics of Responsibility* (Schocken, 2007), 9
112	University of Nebraska Foundation, "Buffett Gives Students Some Priceless Advice" May 29, 2013

WISDOM

113	Ecclesiastes 7:1
114	1 Kings 3:9
115	Shir Hashirim Rabbah, chapter 1, 1:9
116	Babylonian Talmud, Nedarim 41a
117	Babylonian Talmud, Eruvin 53b
118	Babylonian Talmud, Nedarim 40a
119	Youtube.com, "Warren Buffett How to turn $40 into $5 million"
120	Babylonian Talmud, Shabbos 32b
121	Warren Buffett, Lecture, University of Nebraska
122	Pirkei Avot 6:9
123	Pirkei Avot 2:8

CAUTION

| 124 | Rabbi Moses Chaim Luzzatto, *The Path of the Just: Mesillas Yesharim With a New Translation and Shoulder Captions*, translated by Rabbi Yosef Leibler, (Feldheim, 2004), 14 |

125	Annual Letter 1995
126	Annual Letter 2012
127	Owner's Manual
128	Annual Letter 2013
129	Proverbs 22:3
130	Luzzatto, *The Path of the Just*, 19
131	Numbers 21:27
132	Pirkei Avot 2:1
133	Lowenstein, *Buffett*, 134
134	Lowenstein, *Buffett*, 295
135	Pirkei Avot 2:1
136	Babylonian Talmud, Sukkah 52a
137	Proverbs 28:14

FRUGALITY

138	Pirkei Avot 4:1
139	Youtube.com "Interview with Warren Buffett on Buying Iskar with Yaakov Eilon"
140	Lowenstein, *Buffett*, 188
141	Charlie Munger, *Vice Chairman's Thoughts–Past and Future*, www.BerkshireHathaway.com
142	Genesis 32:25
143	Babylonian Talmud, Hulin 91a
144	Franklin, *Autobiography*, 103
145	Leviticus 19:18
146	Bunim, *Ethics from Sinai*, vol.2, 8
147	Proverbs 11:17
148	Shmot Rabbah 9:10
149	Annual Letter 1998

HUMILITY

150	Annual Letter 1996
151	Pirkei Avot 2:5
152	Babylonian Talmud, Brachot 29a

153   Annual Letter 1997

154   Warren Buffett, *Berkshire–Past, Present, and Future,* www.BerkshireHathaway.com

155   Warren Buffett, *The Superinvestors of Graham and Doddsville*

156   Annual Letter 2010

157   Deuteronomy 8:17-18

158   Schroeder, *Snowball*, 641

159   Warren Buffett, *Berkshire–Past, Present, and Future,* www.BerkshireHathaway.com

160   Exodus 18:25

161   Numbers 1

162   Numbers 20:2

163   Judges 3:30

164   Psalms 51:5

165   Annual Letter 1995

166   Proverbs 16:18

167   Proverbs 3:34

JUSTICE

168   Annual Letter 2014

169   Lowenstein, *Buffett*, 144

170   *A Buffett Fortune Fades in Brooklyn: Case of Othmer Gift to Ailing Hospital is Cautionary Tale to Wealthy Donors,* Wall Street Journal, July 19, 2013

171   Babylonian Talmud, Bava Kama 16b

172   Lowenstein, *Buffett*, 144

173   Annual Letter 1992

174   Lowenstein, *Buffett*, 144

175   Schroeder, *Snowball*, 768

176   Youtube.com, "Michael Steinhardt Blasts Warren Buffett" April 5, 2011

177   Leviticus 25:35

178   Babylonian Talmud, Ketubot 67b

179   Carrol Loomis, *A Conversation With Warren Buffett*, Fortune Magazine, June 25, 2006.

180   Babylonian Talmud, Brachot 18b

181	Youtube.com, "Michael Steinhardt Blasts Warren Buffett" April 5, 2011
182	Youtube.com "Interview with Warren Buffett on Buying Iskar with Yaakov Eilon"
183	Babylonian Talmud, Ketubot 63b
184	Deuteronomy 33:4

KINDNESS

185	Annual Letter 1979
186	Annual Letter 1985
187	Annual Letter 1985
188	Lowenstein, *Buffett*, 256
189	Deuteronomy 6:18
190	Leviticus 19:1
191	Nachmanides commentary to Leviticus 19:1
192	Pirkei Avot 5:13
193	Babylonian Talmud, Bava Metzia 30b
194	Proverbs 11:17
195	Babylonian Talmud, Ketubot 67b
196	Babylonian Talmud, Bava Metzia 62a
197	Pirkei Avot 1:14
198	Annual Letter 1985
199	Meir Tamari, *With All Your Possessions: Jewish Ethics and Economic Life*, (Jason Aronson, 1998), 2
200	Joseph B. Schechterman, *Fighter and Prophet the Vladimir Jabotinsky Story: The Last Years*, (A.S.Barnes, 1961), 243
201	Psalms 89:3

HONESTY

202	Annual Letter 1993
203	Annual Letter 1993
204	Schroeder, *Snowball*, 721
205	Annual Letter 2007
206	Youtube.com, "Warren Buffett How to turn $40 into $5 million"
207	Genesis 31:40

208	Luzzatto, *Path of the Just*, 59	
209	Annual Letter 1988	
210	Genesis 25:27	
211	Annual Letter 1995	
212	Annual Letter 1995	
213	Lowenstein, *Buffett*, 383	
214	Original source unknown	
215	Lowenstein, *Buffett*, 395	
216	1 Samuel 15	
217	2 Samuel 12	
218	Lowenstein, *Buffett*, 385	
219	*Poor Charlie's Almanac*, 17	
220	Mishnah Shekalim 3:2	
221	Numbers 32:22	
222	Lowenstein, *Buffett*, 395	
223	Babylonian Talmud, Brachot 28b	
224	Babylonian Talmud, Shabbat 113a	
225	Pirkei Avot 3:1	
226	*Poor Charlie's Almanac*, 19	
227	Proverbs 3:16	
228	Proverbs 28:24	
229	Midrash Rabbah 31:5	
230	Annual Letter 2000	

SILENCE

231	Pirkei Avot 3:17	
232	Babylonian Talmud, Megillah 18a	
233	Schroeder, *Snowball*, 18–19	
234	Youtube.com, "Warren Buffett How to turn $40 into $5 million"	
235	Babylonian Talmud, Sukkah 52b	
236	Youtube.com, "Warren Buffett How to turn $40 into $5 million"	
237	Proverbs 1:11–15	
238	Psalms 34:15	
239	Youtube.com, "Warren Buffett How to turn $40 into $5 million"	
240	James Clavell, *Shogun*, (Mass Market Paperbacks, 1986), 619	

241 Pirkei Avot 1:17
242 Leviticus 19:18
243 Warren Buffett, Original source unknown
244 Lowenstein, *Buffett*, 200
245 Youtube.com, "Warren Buffett How to turn $40 into $5 million"

INVESTING IN VALUES
246 Youtube.com, "Warren Buffett speaks to UGA students"
247   Deuteronomy 8:3
248 Psalms 112:3
249 Owner's Manual

CPSIA information can be obtained at www.ICGtesting.com
Printed in the USA
LVOW11s1155080416

482759LV00001B/201/P